Bank
Strategic Management
and Marketing

Bank Strategic Management and Marketing

Derek F. Channon

Professor of Marketing
International Banking Centre
Manchester Business School,
Manchester, UK

JOHN WILEY & SONS
Chichester · New York · Brisbane · Toronto . Singapore

Library of Congress Cataloging-in-Publication Data:

Channon, Derek F.
  Bank strategic management and marketing.
  Includes index.
  1. Bank management.   2. Bank marketing.   I. Title
HG1615.C46   1985   332.1′068   85-20182
ISBN 0 471 90383 3

British Library Cataloguing in Publication Data:

Channon, Derek F.
  Bank strategic management and marketing.
  1. Banks and banking—Planning
  2. Strategic planning
  I. Title
  332.1′068′4   HG1616.P5/

ISBN 0 471 90383 3

Typeset by Activity Ltd, Salisbury, Wiltshire
Printed and bound in Great Britain

Contents

Preface

This book and its accompanying casebook have developed over a number of years largely as a result of the development of the International Banking Centre at the Manchester Business School and from work undertaken with many individual banks. The banking industry is presently undergoing a revolution world wide. Due to the twin impacts of deregulation and technology an industry that even quite recently in many countries operated as a relatively undifferentiated cartel is now learning to operate in a much more competitive environment. Under such competitive conditions marketing and the process of strategic management suddenly become much more important.

The banking and financial services industry thus provides a fascinating area to observe the effects of rapid industrial structure change. The introduction and use a marketing and strategic management concepts are important ingredients in this change process. However, it has been our experience that such concepts need to be adjusted specifically for the industry and this has been the intent in the case of this book. There is also an accompanying casebook, all the material in which was developed from real banking situations, and disguise has been used to the minimum. Given the relative secrecy of the industry we would like to thank sincerely all those banks who have kindly released material for publication.

The text for the book is based on experience in the areas of marketing and strategic management and how these concepts can be specifically applied to the banking industry. Similarly all the cases in the casebook have been classroom tested with bankers at Manchester and around the world. We hope that both text and the case books will provide a useful contribution to the area of management education for banking.

In its preparation we have received much support from many bankers and banks. We would very much like to thank all those who have helped us. In addition I would like to thank my colleagues at the International Banking Centre and especially its Director, Dr Jim Byrne. I must also thank my research assistants who have helped collect and prepare data used in the cases. In particular thanks are due to John Desmond, Sally Falshawe and Makoto Showda. My secretary Avril Rathbone has also been responsible for much help in preparing the manuscript and I would like to thank her for patience and efficiency. Finally, while the work is the result of the efforts of many, any errors that may occur are regretted, with the responsibility being solely mine.

DEREK F. CHANNON
Manchester Business School
June, 1985

CHAPTER 1

Introduction

1.1 CHANGING PATTERNS OF BANK STRATEGY

The world banking industry has been changing rapidly since the end of the 1960s. During the 1970s the industry in the developed countries of the world experienced a substantial change in competitive conditions as a result of a number of factors. First, the industry tended to go international, led by the leading US money center banks. This resulted in market interpenetration by established overseas competitors and led to substantial challenges to existing indigenous banks, notably in the corporate market. Moreover, the new entrants brought with them new approaches to servicing corporate accounts, while the growing internationalization of the large corporations from all the developed countries led in turn to customer demand for new banking services to meet the specific needs of multicountry operations.

Secondly, new capital markets opened which transformed the traditional patterns of funding for both banks and corporations. By the end of the 1970s large percentages of bank deposits were being provided by funds from other banks *via* the interbank market and the burgeoning growth of the deregulated Euromarkets. Initially centered on London, the Euromarkets had evolved as the world's largest capital market, operating in an increasing number of major financial centers around the world. Moreover, the instruments available within the market had developed to provide a wide range of sophisticated products meeting more or less any specific financial need in a growing variety of currencies or currency combinations.

Third, in response to competition, indigenous banks in Europe reacted and began to build up their own multinational presence, attacking notably the US domestic market, where *via* aquisitions and new openings, they brought their own brand of counterattack to the US indigenous banks with significant success in many cases. Here it was the US banks that were on the receiving end of an aggressive attack which some believed to be unfair, in that the regulations affecting the new competitors appeared to give them advantages on interstate branching and the like which were denied to US domestic banks.

1

Next, the banking industry, despite the constraints of banking law in many countries, began to diversify. Again in the USA the constrictive corset of Glass Steagall prevented a number of the moves that banks were able to undertake in some other countries, but in general commercial banks moved into the areas of asset-based finance, consumer credit finance, merchant banking, trust and pension management, Eurocurrency operations and syndications, credit cards and the like, while at the same time proliferating the range of products offered in conventional banking services. Where legal constraints did not apply, further areas for diversification included insurance broking and underwriting, travel, securities management and computer services. As a result, by the end of the 1970s banks had become more complex in the range of services offered while competitive pressures had eroded margins on commercial lending such that fee-based services were becoming of increasing importance.

Fifth, the industry was identified, largely because of the regulatory constraints, by a growing number of non-banks as being especially attractive to corporations with potential operating advantages in specific areas of activity. Thus, automobile companies such as General Motors, which had long been engaged in dealer and personal finance for automobile purchase, saw the opportunity to extend leasing and credit finance business to non-General Motors customers. Travel card companies like American Express saw the opportunity to offer a variety of financial services to its existing account-holders at little additional cost. And retail companies like Sears Roebuck saw its established chain of nationwide retail outlets as an obvious point of sale for a range of interstate financial services which banks were inhibited from providing.

Sixth, technology began to affect the banking industry. Most notably this appeared in retail banking as, faced with a mounting tide of paper and rising administrative costs, banks turned to plastic cards and electronic machinery in an effort to maintain their ability to handle an increase in transaction volume while controlling costs. Further, the need to provide increased service, especially outside opening hours, led to the increased use of first cash dispensers and later automated teller machines. Similarly, the back office gradually became more automated and from the operations centres of many banks the possibility of selling information-processing services began to emerge as a potential new product market in its own right.

In retail banking too, competition increased. Savings and loan banks initiated the interest-bearing transaction account to bring them into direct competition with commercial banks. Outside the USA, savings banks and building societies also offered a growing range of services to attract small depositors. Larger depositors were lured by the attraction of money market funds or by the development of new sophisticated integrated financial service products such as the Merrill Lynch Cash Management Account. In retail lending, competition also increased. Credit card companies, collectively owned and operated by banks, offered easy credit, stores offered retail revolving systems, credit finance companies offered loans for specialized assets, second mortgages and the like.

By the end of the 1970s, therefore, the banking industry had become much more competitive. The traditional demarcation lines between the classes of financial institutions were rapidly breaking down, while a number of major competitors were operating on a global scale rather than as the regional or national competitors they had been previously. Moreover, many new market entrants were emerging which, uninhibited by the legal constraints of the industry established as appropriate for an earlier age, allowed the newcomers a competitive advantage. Finally, new technology and substitute products threatened the traditional mode of banking operations.

1.2 BANKING IN THE 1980s

While change within the banking industry in the 1970s was very rapid, the 1980s seem likely to bring an acceleration in the pace of this change. Amongst the trends discernible for the present decade are the following.

1.2.1 Retail Banking

(a) Increased segmentation of consumer groups

A number of segments are already emerging as being especially important such as:

The rich. A growing number of banks are establishing or are operating specialist private banking units to provide a customized service for personal clients with assets available for investment or management of over $100,000. Such units are often located in no- or low-tax areas and build upon the traditional secrecy and personal service long practised by the Swiss banks.

HNWIs. Below the level of the very rich, a segment has been developed to cater for the special needs of those individuals of moderate wealth. Making use of sophisticated computer systems, Merrill Lynch introduced its Cash Management Account to provide an effective money market interest rate for deposits of $20,000 or more coupled with a Visa card and checking account and the ability to generate loans automatically based on the value of securities contained in the account. The rapid success of this type of account has forced banks to respond and offer interest on current account balances at money market rates, while other securities companies have entered the market with similar products to that of Merrill Lynch. As a result, the traditional deposit base of the commercial banks has been substantially eroded.

Account Stratification. In response to attacks on their traditional deposit base, banks have begun to interrogate their existing account base with the view to identifying accounts with potential for various specific services such as personal loans, credit finance, insurance, first and second mortgages, insurance or deposits. There will also be strong pressure to discard the unprofitable segments of most banks' retail customer base.

(b) Replacement of Paper-Based Systems

The trend of the 1970s toward machine banking is increasing as banks work to reduce the cost of consumer banking using bricks-and-mortar branches and human resources. Not only is the growth of more sophisticated automated teller machines occurring but the development of home banking seems likely by the end of the decade. At the same time, credit and debit cards are expected to continue to grow and offer an increasing range of services as more information is contained on a card in the striping or in an inbuilt microchip. The substitution of machinery for human labor will continue and probably accelerate as the relative cost of new technology delivery systems falls while that of human tellers and back office personnel continues to rise.

(c) Increased competition for both deposits and loans

The pattern of increased competition between banks and other institutions providing financial service to consumers experienced at the end of the 1970s will continue. In the United States interstate banking will become finally established, with large money center banks entering other states, especially in growth areas of the country such as the Sun Belt and the south-west. At the same time interstate card systems shared by multibank organizations can be expected in an effort to counter the moves by out-of-state banks. In states such as California and New York foreign banks such as the Japanese and the British will provide growing competition for indigenous organizations.

In addition to the banks, new entrants will continue to penetrate against selected retail market segments. The pattern established by Merrill Lynch will be repeated by all major securities companies in combination with banks or other institutions such as insurance companies, American Express and the like. Similarly, retail groups like Sears Roebuck with a natural synergy with financial services due to an established customer base and distribution coverage may be expected to increase their threat to traditional bank business.

The patterns of competitive behavior in the USA will be similarly repeated in many other countries. In the UK, additional competition can be expected from securities companies, building societies, foreign banks and retailers. In Germany, late to introduce card-based systems, the savings banks, foreign banks, card companies and retailers can be expected to increase competition. In Japan the securities companies and the Post Office offer the greatest threat to the commercial banks.

1.2.2 Wholesale Banking

(c) Continued Intensive Competition

The intensive competition that developed in the 1970s will continue and even increase during the 1980s as banks increasingly strive for competitive advantage and in so doing tend to cancel out one another's efforts.

As multinational corporations find they increasingly need banks less as they add internally the skills traditionally provided by banks and demand ever lower rates for money, banks themselves are turning their attention to the 'middle market'. In so doing, however, they are forcing interest rates down in this sector for attractive accounts while reducing customer loyalty as the companies adopt multibank relationships. Smaller banks such as South East and Standard Chartered have opted to concentrate on specific services such as trade finance or geographic territories such as the Far East or the Caribbean basin. Other banks like the Texas banks have concentrated on specific areas of lending such as real estate and energy lending.

Further, while the American international banks led the competitive attack in the 1970s, the 1980s have begun with the counter-attack of the large European banks such as Barclays, Banque Nationale de Paris, Credit Lyonnais, Algemene Bank and Deutsche Bank. As these banks build up their global networks to match those of the leading US money center banks or build upon already established branches, the number of major competitors entered in all the major corporate and wholesale business centers will increase to an average of over 50 major banks.

Still to come as major global competitors by the end of the decade are the large Japanese commercial banks and leading specialist banks such as the Industrial Bank of Japan and the Bank of Tokyo. These banks, which are normally at the center of massive industrial groups, can be expected to emerge as extremely powerful and important competitors as their industrial group associates continue to expand overseas and develop the Japanese international economic position. By the mid-1980s the large Japanese banks had already achieved five positions among the top ten global banks.

Finally, a number of new important financial institutions are emerging from the newly industrializing countries and those countries with substantial petrodollar surpluses. Banks such as Banco do Brasil, Hong Kong & Shanghai and those of the Gulf States can be expected to play a greater role in the world of international banking in the future.

(b) Development of Systems Products

In the same way that banks are turning to technology to change their approach to consumer markets, so in the corporate and wholesale markets the development of systems-based products is becoming of increased importance. Making use of their global networks and advanced communications, computer and information processing capabilities, the largest banks are endeavoring to build customer loyalty and fee-based income by offering cash management, and, in future, comprehensive data/information processing services.

(c) Further Competition from Non-Banks

Non-banks such as American Express, Merrill Lynch and the major credit finance companies have already established a significant position in the corporate market and can be expected to continue to do so. In addition, a growing number of industrial companies are broadening the scope of their financial services operations to enter external markets. Thus organizations like General Motors Acceptance Corporation offer industrial credit finance, leasing and the like to companies outside General Motors, many captive insurance companies now legitimately trade with third party organizations, and in the coming decade the emergence of trading companies such as those of Japan can be expected in the West in major corporations like General Electric.

1.3 THE NEED FOR MARKET PLANNING

As a result of the growing level of competition and the rapid pace of change, more and more banks are increasing their strategic planning efforts in an attempt to allocate resources in a way which provides them with a competitive advantage or reduces external threats. At the same time marketing is emerging as an especially important element in bank planning. Traditionally banks have not really paid adequate attention to either strategic planning or marketing and as a consequence most have turned to external consultants or industrial companies for their concepts and methodologies. During the 1970s, however, although banks paid some attention to the new concepts, their main emphasis remained on traditional 'banking' rather than on management skills. The competitive environment of the 1980s is forcing the reappraisal of this position and management skills are growing in importance.

1.4 THE ROLE OF THIS BOOK

While most of the conceptual skills being introduced into banks have their origin in manufacturing industry, it is important to recognize that in many respects banking is a very different industry. As a consequence, a number of the concepts and relationships established in manufacturing may not be wholly applicable in banking or have a different emphasis. This book is therefore devoted to strategic management and marketing in the banking industry, with particular emphasis on international corporate banking. It builds upon the years of work undertaken by the International Banking Centre at the Manchester Business School, probably the largest institution for specialist education in international banking in the world. This work, which has been undertaken in conjunction with many of the world's leading banks, has always been practical in nature and courses have been designed in conjunction with practicing line bankers. We are extremely grateful for all the help and assistance these bankers have provided over the years and hope this may in some small way repay their help.

The text examines techniques of bank strategic planning and marketing based upon working systems in leading banks. In addition, the importance of techniques such as competitor analysis and product development are discussed from a banking perspective. A detailed analysis of corporate financial service purchasing is included to try and emphasize the position of the bank customer. To supplement and reinforce the text a comprehensive collection of up-to-date banking cases is provided in an accompanying casebook. These range from cases outlining various aspects of the strategy of many important named banks and non-banks from around the world to a series of operational cases drawn from the experiences of a number of cooperating banks. Nearly all the material has been tested with line bankers drawn from many countries attending the many programs run by the International Banking Centre, while others have been prepared for specific banks' internal management needs. We hope that you will find the results helpful to your bank.

CHAPTER 2

Bank Strategic Planning

2.1 INTRODUCTION

Strategic planning is an essential ingredient in the process of strategic management of the bank. It results in the development of the bank's long-term objectives and the design of action plans throughout the bank which lead to the achievement of these objectives. Specifically, the bank's strategic plan makes explicit:

- The market priorities, which determine resource allocation
- The assumptions behind the choice of market priorities
- The changes required to capitalize on market opportunities
- The timing of strategic moves
- An estimate of the environment in which the bank will act
- The expected rate of progress in strategy implementation

The plan thus describes the *strategic direction* the bank will take by assigning specific objectives and investment priorities to particular *market segments* in which the bank operates, so committing resources to the *desired mix of businesses* which will result in achievement of the bank's long-term objectives. As a guide to management, the bank's plan also describes the strategies to be pursued in the form of *action plans* leading to changes in *business variables* under the control of management. These variables are the levers which can be manipulated to arrive at the desired strategic position for each bank business. The desired changes themselves define the implementation tasks of managers.

2.2 STRATEGIC PLAN CONTENT

The strategic plan should include the following components.

1. *Mission.* This states the overall purpose or *raison d'être* of the bank. It also applies at the level of the organizational subunit, stating in addition the nature of activities and any self-imposed constraints.

8

2. *Objectives.* These are usually measurable characteristics and their future value should be stated. Typically, objectives are cited for variables such as financial return, size, efficiency and service quality.
3. *Environment/market assumptions.* These contain explicit statements about future trends in strategic market segments in which the bank participates together with factors which may affect these trends or impact upon the bank's organization or its freedom to act.
4. *Competitive strength evaluation.* The plan should explicitly assess the bank's relative strengths and weaknesses for specific factors such as market share, service quality and relative costs.
5. *Assessment of opportunity.* For each market segment, the plan should assess threats to and opportunities for the achievement of mission and objectives on the basis of the environment and market assumptions and relative competitive strength.
6. *Market portfolio strategy.* This ingredient identifies the desired investment strategies for each of the markets in which bank units participate and the objectives to be attained for each.
7. *Strategic changes in controllable factors.* Objectives and goals for action plans stating changes in capabilities or resources under the control of unit management and selected as most likely for achieving the desired market results.
8. *Action plans for change implementation.* Specific programs including measurable goals, events and timing which will result in the changes specified in action plan objectives.
9. *Expected financial results.* These indicate the anticipated financial outcome in terms of revenue, profits and return on assets for the units.

The plan also needs to be developed for each organizational level of the bank. The normal starting point for bank analysis is the individual market segment. However, the bank's organization structure may affect the responsibilities for making changes in market strategic variables. Further, organization structure itself is a major variable under management control, and indeed it turns out to be a key factor for bank differentiation. For major international banks the question of market and business unit definition can be difficult to resolve, due to conflicting claims of product and geography. In practice country units are logical organizational planning centers, but for products and/or customers which span national boundaries coordination or planning control should focus on the customer/product segment. The differences between plan content at various organizational levels are illustrated in Figure 2.1.

2.3 THE PROCESS OF BANK PLANNING

The process of bank strategy planning at the corporate level is illustrated in Figure 2.2. At the corporate level it begins with an assessment of mission and

Figure 2.1
Hierarchical Bank Plan Requirements

	Corporate level	Division level	Market segment level
Mission	Corporate mission	Markets, activities assigned to div. constraints	Scope of activities assigned to develop market segment
Objectives	Corporate objectives	Div. objectives supporting corp. objective	Segment objective
Assumptions	Specific to corp. capabilities, opportunities, threats	Specific to scope of div. Activities	Specific to mkt demand Competition, service, ...
Competitive strength	Corp. strength, weakness	Div. strength, weakness	Specific share, strength, weakness
Assessment of market opportunity		As evaluated and reviewed at all levels	
Market portfolio strategy	Overall, corp. mix & priority, including new areas of interest	Mix for mkts assigned to div.	Specific investment priority for this segment
Changes desired in controllable variables	Attack plans for change in corp. capabilities Specific to corp.	Attack plan for change in div. capabilities Specific to div. capabilities	Attack plans to change factors Specific to this segment
Programs to implement change			Specific to segment
Expected financial results	Corp. financial measures	Div. financial measures	Segment financial measures

Figure 2.1   Hierarchical bank plan requirements

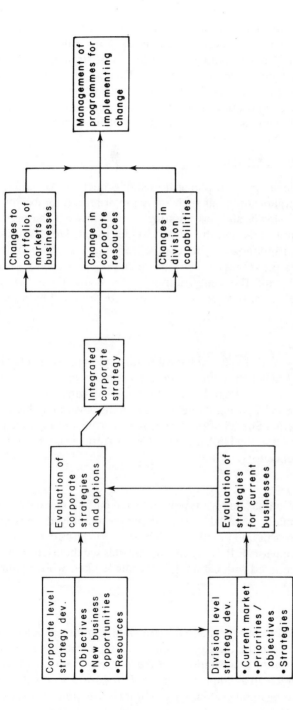

Figure 2.2 The process of bank corporate planning

objectives, which are matched against opportunities and resources. At the departmental or divisional level current market priorities, objectives and strategies are evaluated and compared with corporate strategies and options to develop an integrated corporate strategy. This in turn indicates desired changes in the positions of the bank's business portfolio, in its levels and direction of resource allocation and in organizational capabilities. These are ultimately translated into action programs for implementing the changes.

2.3.1 Setting the Bank Mission

The first stage in developing the plan is the establishment of the bank's mission statement. Each organization has such a mission or reason for existence. This only changes very slowly and has a major impact on what the organization chooses to do or not to do and the way it decides to act. Understanding your own bank's mission and those of your competitors is an important ingredient in establishing successful strategies, by recognizing the constraints within your own organization and the opportunities offered by those within your competitors'. The actual mission of the bank is determined by a number of factors:

Corporate history
The past history of the bank will have a significant impact on behavior. Past successes will influence the choice of future directions whilst past failures will tend to lead to areas of avoidance. The bank's origins will also affect its position in relation to particular geographic areas, customer classes, and so on. Hong Kong and Shanghai Bank thus sees its zone of influence to be the Pacific Basin and also the USA and UK; Credit Agricole is strongly attached to its farming depositors.

Corporate culture
Every organization has its own unique internal culture made up of the way things are normally done, the type of people employed and the set of organizational norms and practices which condition and govern both formal and informal behavior. J. P. Morgan bankers thus see themselves as financial consultants, compared with Citibank corporate bankers who are much more lending-oriented.

Power structure
The power structure of the bank will significantly influence behaviour. This again applies to both the formal and informal organization structure. Thus, for example, despite protestations to the contrary, not all executives in Barclays are perceived as equal, especially if they are descended from one of the bank's founding families. Similarly, a branch-oriented bank such as Bank of America tends to structure its activities around geography, by comparison

with most of its New York-based competitors where organization around customers is more usual.

Key decision-makers
The style, aspirations and values of key decision-makers have a significant effect on the basic purpose of the bank. Virtually no major shifts in strategy or organization occur without a prior change of leadership, and this is normally a prerequisite for any attempt to shift the organizational purpose. For example, the recent change in the strategic direction of Chase Manhattan and First Chicago Corporation required such a change of leadership.

The basic mission of the bank can thus act as a serious deterrent to shifts in strategy but usually represents a deep strength providing some overall distinctive competence which can be built upon for the development of future strategy. It must, however, be recognized that to change a basic organizational purpose is usually very difficult and takes a significant time. Strategies which expect to make such changes quickly are therefore unlikely to be realistic. This concept of overall purpose for the bank needs to be identified and set down in an overall corporate mission statement. The statement sets out the overall direction the bank wishes to pursue and identifies the nature of the activities it will engage in and self-imposed constraints that may apply as a result of history, culture and management values.

2.3.2 Setting Objectives

The second stage of developing the overall bank plan is the setting of objectives. These are set by top management, taking into account the potential of the external environment, any self-imposed constraints identified by the overall mission statement, the internal resources of the bank and the requirements of external shareholders as shown in Figure 2.3.

The corporate objectives usually remain relatively stable over the medium term and should consist of quantified variables, although many banks also include non-quantified objectives. Later in the planning process at other levels within the bank, strategic groups, divisions or departments will also set out their own mission statements and objectives as part of the detailed bank plan. In evaluating the objectives of the bank and its operating units it is extremely important to check that they are internally consistent and that the achievement of one does not automatically exclude the achievement of another. All too often internal consistency is missing. Similarly, in reviewing the overall plan check that the objectives of the operating units are consistent with those of the bank as a whole. Again it is common to find inconsistencies. One often encountered is that operating units will still be seeking to grow their businesses while the bank, as part of its market portfolio strategy, might actually require

14

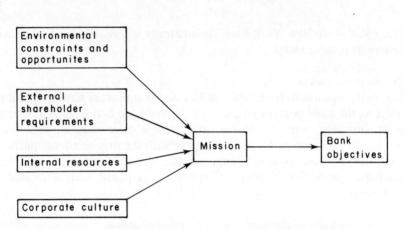

Figure 2.3 The relationship between bank mission and objectives

some businesses to contract in order to generate the resources required for other elements in the portfolio to grow. In the event that inconsistencies are identified in the bank's objectives, aim to remove them by checking which objectives are paramount.

2.3.3 Market Definition

The next stage in developing the bank strategic plan is strategy development. The first step in this is to assess, and order, potential market opportunities as shown in Figure 2.4. A market is defined as an intersection between a class of customers and a bank product or service group. Defining the markets the bank is engaged in is actually a very difficult task and requires a substantial degree of creative effort. In practice, virtually no bank endeavors to service all the needs of all potential customers. Instead the bank operates in a series of 'served' markets, each of which is a subset of the total market as illustrated in Figure 2.5. The concept of 'served' market breaks down the total market to that segment or segments to which the bank will purposively try and sell products or services.

Each market the bank is engaged in, therefore, should be sufficiently defined such that you can answer each of the following questions:

- Who precisely are the customers?
- What are their needs?
- What products or services of the bank meet these needs?
- Can we provide these efficiently, profitably and at an acceptable level of risk?
- What resources does the bank need to deliver these services?
- How will the bank manage these resources?

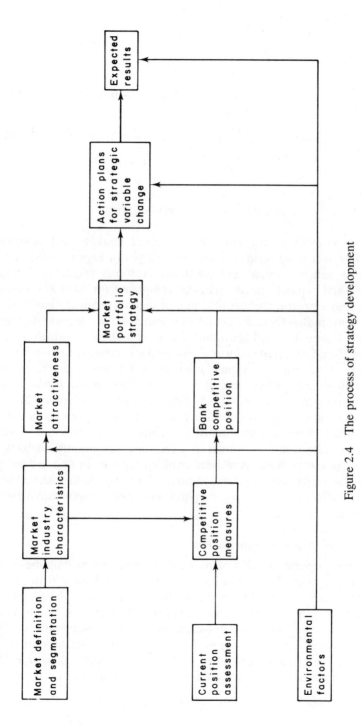

Figure 2.4   The process of strategy development

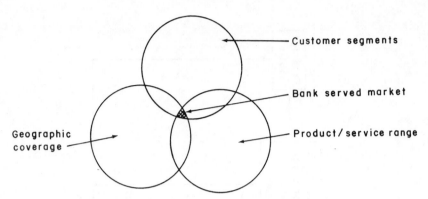

Figure 2.5 Served market definition

In order to evaluate the potential of served markets first complete a customer/product needs grid such as those shown in Figure 2.6(a) and (b). In practice, both corporate and consumer customer segments should be subdivided and separate needs matrices completed for each key customer class. The more precise the identification of market segment boundaries the better but ensure that these are actually meaningful. An adequate description of a market segment should constitute a set of boundaries to which strategies can be specifically targeted and where a defendable position can ultimately be established. Note the geographic boundaries for many of these served markets will differ sharply, and it is not uncommon for banks to offer different geographic served markets to different customer classes. Thus many banks will provide certain worldwide services to large corporate accounts and to some others from specific industry sectors, while services to average consumers will be usually confined to a local area or country. A bank like Chase Manhattan provides consumer banking services in and around New York but offers a worldwide service to private banking clients with deposits of over $100,000 and to large corporations with international service requirements.

2.3.4 Corporate Market Segmentation

For the large corporate market plans are created mainly by building up from the marketing plans for individual accounts (see Chapter 6 on account marketing planning), while for those larger groups of customers and prospects marketing planning is based on aggregate strategies. Middle market corporate accounts are usefully planned by a combination of these techniques, using improved segmentation screening variables to initiate marketing plans supplemented by individual account plans for those organizations whose potential, based on the screening criteria, justifies the expense.

Corporate markets

Local MNCs
Foreign MNCs
Aerospace cos
Transport cos
Trading cos
Energy cos
Consumer product cos
Engineering cos
Construction cos
Property cos
Shipping cos
Insurance cos
Correspondent banks
Other financial instns
Retailers
Government
State & local authorities
State enterprises
Other middle markets
Region A
Region B
Region C
Small business markets
Region A
Region B
Region C

Products:

Local checking accounts
Local deposit services
Local overdraft
Local term loans
Acceptance credits
Export finance
Import finance
Standby LCs
Foreign drafts
Local collections
Local leasing
Local factoring
Cash management services
Treasury advice services
Credit card services
House purchase loans
Investment advice
Trustee services
International currency lending
Loan syndications
International investment advice
Mergers and acquisitions
Foreign trade services
Project finance
Foreign exchange services
Bonds & private placements
Wage payments
Foreign subsidiary finance
International cash management
Buyer credits
Construction loans
Venture capital
Computer services
Machine banking
Tax advice
Pension management
Insurance broking
Data processing

Figure 2.6(a) Bank market corporate customer/product needs matrix

Consumer markets	Local checking accounts	Local deposit accounts	Children's accounts	Term deposit accounts	Overdraft loans	Mortgage loans	Credit finance loans	Education loans	Personal loans	Second mortgages	Investment advice	Tax services	Trustee services	Life insurance	Non-life insurance	Credit cards	Travellers' checks	Other travel services	Small business loans	Venture capital	Pension advice	Machine banking	Accounting advice	Security deposit services	International credits
Very rich private banking																									
Middle market private banking																									
HNWIs																									
Professionals																									
Self-employed																									
Students/young bachelors																									
Young marrieds																									
Full-nest marrieds																									
White-collar, older marrieds																									
Retirees																									
Savings-conscious																									

Figure 2.6(b) Bank market retail customer/product needs matrix

Useful variables for this initial approach to market segmentation include:

Turnover
Turnover provides a simple crude means of segmentation. For example: Some banks determine their mode of organization based upon turnover measures such as accounts above $100m turnover being handled by a director or senior vice president; some international banks will not pursue accounts of less than $50m sales.

Turnover gives an indication of the size of business available for many products and is perhaps the widest used single segmentation variable. However, most banks when designing key account target lists make overuse of this variable without coupling it with other factors such as geography, probability of dislodging a competitor, etc. As a result, many banks are pursuing the same key accounts and often neglecting potentially more profitable and more readily penetrable accounts with perhaps a somewhat lower volume of total business. *The largest apparent volume segment is seldom the easiest to penetrate or the most profitable.*

Turnover is also an important variable when used in conjunction with others to create ratios. However, remember turnover is not an available measure in many service and public sector organizations.

Geography
Corporate accounts in fact tend to be geographically clustered. Geography can thus be used as a variable to decide upon the allocation of business development resources, new branches, etc., and for assessing market potential within particular regions.

Industry classification
This is a somewhat difficult variable to use, since many companies are very diversified and operate in a number of product market areas. Crude industry measures are, however, useful both in terms of assigning account responsibilty and developing specific products. For example, insurance broking companies and commodity traders would be especially interested in rapid money transfer systems. Industry specialization by account executives is a real alternative to a geographic branch-based system of business development, and even if not practised it is important for bank executives to learn about the specific financial needs of key industries.

Competitor bank relationship
One of the most useful segmentation variables is 'Who does an account bank with at present?' From this knowledge it is possible to conduct competitor analysis to assess your relative strengths and weaknesses compared with your competitor and attack the account with those services you are especially

good at. Remember, whenever you take new business, it has to come either from growth in the overall market or from a competitor.

Subsidiary structure

The majority of larger companies or industrial groups consist of different subsidiaries and/or are multisite operations. It may be possible to gain an early foothold at an account by taking business at a subsidiary or specific plant. The decision process for bank appointments can rely heavily on the attitude of subsidiary units, especially for some services, and this may therefore represent a significant potential route for building a lead bank relationship. It is, however, important to understand the decision process for banking appointments before spending too long trying to gain business at a subsidiary of a larger group.

Number of employees

A useful indicator of organization size, this can also be used to indicate sensitivity to wage demands, and when taken in conjunction with other factors provides a number of useful derived variables such as value added per employee, capital employed per employee, etc. It can be used in the design of service packages incorporating personal services, which often form a suitable starting point for account penetration.

Level of export sales

This is an important indicator of the level of international activity, both in absolute size and also when used as a percentage of turnover to indicate the relative importance of this. An obvious indicator for forex and acceptance credit business, it may also point to network matching possibilities, multicurrency lending, confirming business, and the like.

Number and location of overseas offices and subsidiaries

This is another indicator of the level of multinational activity. It is also useful for network matching against the bank's own overseas network and with reference to the location of specific branches.

Current assets

Subdivided into major components, with stocks and debtors being singled out for specific attention, these indicate managerial ability when compared with industry averages, degree of working capital intensity, and the like. They also suggest specific types of banking service such as factoring, overdraft lending, acceptance credits, transaction services, and the like.

Current liabilities

Subdivided into major components, with creditors and short debt being singled out for specific attention, these indicate debt capacity level and managerial control over creditors.

Fixed assets
Subdivided into property and plant and equipment for use in security evaluation and identification of capital funding needs and capital intensity, fixed assets can be usefully examined to explore financing opportunities in all forms including leasing commercial paper and the like.

Interest paid
Subdivided into long and short interest, this, in conjunction with earnings, indicates capacity to repay lending. Short interest should be checked against actual year-end balance-sheet short debt to identify seasonal overdraft requirements.

Long and short debt
Used on their own and as a component in debt/equity and other financial ratios, these indicate debt requirements and capacity. They may also indicate specific service opportunities such as the conversion of short to term debt or leasing possibilities.

Profitability
Several versions are used. EBIT indicates absolute level of earnings, also used in conjunction with other variables to indicate gross margin and return on investment.

Earnings before tax may also be used on its own and as a measure of ROI. Earnings after tax indicates levels of tax paid. Industry average is useful as an indicator of tax saving potential, managerial capability and corporate viabilty.

In markets where suitable data are available, the preliminary screening of corporate accounts can be usefully computerized and coupled with basic credit assessment to evaluate market potential and relative risk.

In practice, using only one or two segmentation variables is usually ineffective. For example, a bank might identify all multinational accounts over $250m turnover as key accounts and devote the bulk of its business development effort to penetrating these. Yet, if the bank does not have the specialist services and skills required by this type of account it will often be wasting its resources. Instead it might be better off attacking high export oriented, medium sized companies selling mainly to Eastern Europe and the developed countries and needing specialist foreign exchange and export credit services if these are areas the bank is well equipped to service.

In order to home in on a narrow market segment, therefore, banks should make use of several variables at the same time. This is where computerization proves most helpful, since from a data base this can be done very quickly. Usually employing three or four of these indicators or ratios derived from them, it is possible to subdivide the corporate market into very small segments which can be assigned priorities and attacked systematically. In addition, it is possible to monitor your own accounts to assess the impact of changing market conditions and to identify possible targets which your competitors might seek to exploit.

For example, your bank might be interested in accounts with an overall level of sales of more than $50m, exports of more than $8m, a debt/equity ratio of not more than 50 per cent and interest cover of at least five times. In most countries the number of accounts fulfilling this set of criteria would actually be extremely small and could be quickly isolated and serviced.

2.3.5 Retail Market Segmentation

In addition to the need to segment the corporate model, there is a growing requirement in banks to look carefully at their retail account base and aim at segmenting this with the view to isolating special groups of customers particularly suited to specific products or services. The traditional method used has been to segregate out high net worth individuals or the rich and offer a special service to this group. However, today this group has in turn been subdivided further, as follows:

Superich
Customers with a deposit capability or net worth of $1 million and above. While such individuals are seen as a primary source of relatively low-cost deposits, they are also attractive prospects for investment management services, tax advice, insurance and large loans.

Private banking group
These customers are similar to the first group but in some banks a lower cutoff is established at, say, $100,000 or more. Again these individuals are a primary source of deposits and require investment and taxation advice. They may also be candidates for lending.

HNWI
Today this segment is virtually a mass market group. They provide a substantial element of the endowment in current account balances and have for years been neglected by traditional banks, who have offered low or no interest on deposits. This group has been the principal segment attacked by money market funds, Amex Gold Card and Merrill Lynch with dramatic success, causing a massive drain on bank deposits in the USA, especially for savings and loan banks. It is not merely a source of deposits, however: its members are also active purchasers of investment management services, insurance, travel services, large mortgages and other loan products. Banks will have to look carefully at this customer group in the coming years to try to

win them back from the attractive package of financial services offered by the broking houses.

Professionals

This group of specialist, professionally qualified self-employed such as dentists, doctors, lawyers and accountants are attractive prospects not merely because of their net worth but also as good potential for small business loans, data processing and pension planning services, which need to be carefully packaged to meet their specific needs. Thus, although they overlap with the HNWI group, they form a specific subsegment which can be addressed separately.

Self-employed

A wider segment than the professional group and usually associated with higher risk lending, this group is also attractive not only for loan services but for insurance pension planning, tax advice and possibly data processing.

Students

A large number of banks make specialized marketing appeals to students in the expectation that capturing their accounts at this stage will ultimately leave the bank with valuable up-market accounts after the student graduates. Regrettably, this anticipated long-term loyalty is breaking down as other banks attempt to provide specialist services to postgraduation groups such as professionals.

Senior citizens

A generally neglected segment until recently, senior citizens actually have a high propensity to save. A number of savings and loan banks have found that this segment can be kept very loyal by providing specialist services such as group travel, social events and the like to meet a real need for companionship often felt by such customers.

Youth

Many banks are attempting to generate loyalty very early by picking off the child and youth market. This forms a significant small savings market in aggregate, which banks have attempted to attract with offers of higher interest rates and free gifts.

Conventional market research techniques for segmentation can also be used to attack the consumer market. These would involve both demographic and psychographic variables. As a first step your bank might stratify its accounts using consumer demographics and bank data such as average balances and transaction rates to identify if the accounts are profitable. As a rule high deposit, low transaction accounts are very profitable, as are accounts with a substantial loan commitment. The accounts which are unprofitable are those with a low balance and high transaction rate. Some such as student accounts may be tolerated at this stage in the expectation that they will subsequently mature and become attractive. Others can be improved by efforts at service cross-selling, bearing in mind that the type of services required by particular individuals will vary according to demographics and lifestyle. You will also usually find a smaller group of accounts with low balances, a high level of transactions and limited future potential. With these accounts you will have to decide if you can raise the cost of transactions to make them economically viable, encourage the accounts to bank elsewhere or maintain the loss-makers on social grounds. This group of unprofitable accounts may represent some 30 per cent of the average retail customer base. An illustration of consumer segmentation variables and their impact is given in Table 2.1, which shows how lifestyles and demographics have been combined to create consumer segments which account for a known percentage of the population and can be specifically addressed as a part of bank strategy. Such segment sizes and characteristics will of course vary according to location and it is therefore important to conduct detailed market research before adopting specific strategies aimed at individual segments.

Many banks pay insufficient attention to segmentation of either corporate or consumer markets. However, segmentation is crucial to strategic management and will be of paramount importance in the coming decade as banks strive to differentiate themselves in a relatively fragmented and highly competitive marketplace. In these conditions, without specialization and service differentiation, most banking activities will become price-sensitive commodity services with few opportunities for attractive margins.

2.3.6 Market/Industry Characteristics

Having identified the appropriate customer segments for your bank, plot their service usage on the customer/service needs matrix and for each market endeavor to assess the following market/industry characteristics.

Market characteristics
- Market size
- Historic growth rate
- Projected growth rate
- Number of accounts in total
- Number making up 50 per cent and 80 per cent of the market
- Trend in market concentration
- Buying decision process
- Service usage characteristics
- Service delivery process
- Financial characteristics of customers

Service characteristics
- Degree of service differentiation
- Relative capital intensity
- Value added
- Level and type of risk to the bank
- Relative profitabilty of the service
- Rate of service change/innovation
- Details of add-on service characteristics
- Cross-selling potential
- Impact on shared cost structures
- Service integration with other bank services

Competitive characteristics
- Identity of major competitors and their market shares (including non-banks where relevant)
- Bank's market share and relative share
- Changes in number of competitors
- Trends in market share
- Degree of competitor concentration
- Relative service quality (assess the full concept of the service, including delivery, time, accuracy, etc.)
- Relative service price
- Relative service cost
- Relative capital intensity
- Relative marketing effort
- Relative delivery system capability (includes network size and coverage, account officer skill, etc.)
- Relative employee skills
- Relative resource availability
- Relative systems capability
- Barriers to entry or exit

Environmental characteristics
- Economic trends and their impact on the market
- Social trends and their impact
- Political trends and their impact
- Technological trends and their impact

The quality of your plans will be heavily dependent upon the information you use to generate them. The careful selection of information is therefore important. Japanese banks can teach Western banks a great deal about information gathering and analysis, while the intelligence systems developed by their associate trading companies have no parallel amongst Western

Table 2.1

Identifying Bank Market Segments

Cluster I profile (10%) Upper level, white collar	Cluster II profile (18%) New retirees	Cluster III profile (9%) New, blue collar	Cluster IV profile (15%) Price-conscious	Cluster V profile (13%) Savings-conscious, debt avoidance	Cluster VI profile (24%) Older, lower income, blue collar
Most important factors Integrity Ego enhancement Expertise Least important factors Time convenience Location convenience Demographics 45–54 age College grad. or better Upper income Professional/management Teachers Farm owners Financial attitudes Optimistic Less reliant on savings	Most important factors Time convenience Bank philosophy Pricing Least important factors Location convenience Demographics 55+ age Newer residents Middle to upper income Retired Financial attitudes Pessimistic Reliance on savings Not new brand tryers Not heavy users of credit	Most important factors Location convenience Time convenience Least important factors Bank philosophy Ego enhancement Demographics Under 35 age Lower income Blue collar Renters Newer residents Financial attitudes Optimistic No strong need for savings Average use of credit cards Not new brand tryers Not bargain hunters Non-sociable Unfavorable attitude toward banks	Most important factors Time convenience Location convenience Pricing Least important factors Ego enhancement Expertise Bank philosophy Demographics Below 44 age Lower to middle income Large families Financial attitudes Smart shoppers Above-average use of credit cards Negative view of debt	Most important factors Location convenience Bank philosophy Integrity Least important factors Time convenience Pricing Demographics Middle income Financial attitudes Ego Reliance on cash (if possible) Conscious of debt Savings reliance New brand tryers Neutral attitude toward banks Banking habits	Most important factors Location convenience Time convenience Bank philosophy Least important factors Integrity Expertise Demographics 55+ age Lower income Less educated Blue collar, sales/clerical Home owners Long-time residents Financial attitudes Pessimistic Reliance on bank savings Unfavorable attitude toward credit Reliance on cash Smart shoppers Neutral attitude toward banks

Do not shop around	Favorable attitude toward banks	Banking habits	Unfavorable attitude toward banks	High multiple use of financial institutions	Banking habits
Not price-sensitive		Below-average use of all financial institutions except banks		Above-average number of savings accounts	Above-average use of banks
Considered heavy credit card users	Banking habits	Above-average number of credit cards	Banking habits	Above-average number of credit cards	Below-average number of savings accounts, loans, credit cards
Neutral attitude toward banks	Above-average use of credit unions	Above-average in personal loans	High multiple use of financial institutions	Below-average number of personal loans	Satisfied with banking hours (Saturday)
Banking habits	Satisfied with banking hours	Dissatisfied with banking hours	Above-average use of checking, savings, personal loans	Satisfied with current banking hours	Inside bank facilities
Below-average use of savings and loans and credit unions	Media habits	Drive-in	Below-average number of credit cards	Media habits	Media habits
Above-average in number of savings accounts held	Above-average use of radio and TV	Night depositories	Least satisfied with current banking hours	Above-average use of radio and newspapers	High radio use
Above-average in number of loans made		Media habits		Below-average use of TV	
Satisfied with banking hours		Below-average use of media, especially TV			
Media habits					
Below average in use of radio, TV and newspapers					

Source: D. H. Robertson and D. N. Bellenger, Identifying bank market segments, *Journal of Bank Research*, Winter 1977, 280–81.

industrial organizations. Most data required to conduct careful market analysis are available from published sources, including:

- Annual reports
- Industry statistics
- Government consumer statistics
- Newspapers
- Trade magazines
- Industry association reports
- Company newspapers
- Company product literature

Internal resources include:

- Credit assessment reports
- Internal research facilities
- Account officer reports
- Branch/country manager reports
- Commissioned market research
- Consultancy, e.g. hire of retired treasurers, etc.

From the data on each market the relative market attractiveness can be assessed and this, in conjunction with the current position assessment, can be used to clarify the bank's relative competitive position.

2.3.7 Current Position Assessment

Next, from the data collected on the bank's markets and the relative position of the bank, conduct an appraisal of the strengths and weaknesses, threats and opportunities facing the organization. Using the form shown in Figure 2.7, each executive at the corporate strategic sector and business unit level should identify the five most important current strengths and weaknesses and the five most important threats and opportunities facing the bank over the next five years. Each should then complete the cross-impact matrix, indicating how the strengths and weaknesses impact if at all on the threats and opportunities. Where a strength for example can be expected to have a major positive impact on a threat or opportunity, this should be indicated with a score of two pluses as shown, while a large negative impact scores two minuses. Mark no impact with a zero.

This exercise should be conducted periodically throughout the bank at various levels. It is extremely useful in identifying and assessing a number of important issues:

Key strategic issues
By restricting the number of threats and opportunities, strengths and

Present	Cross-impacts										Future
	Opportunities					Threats					Opportunities
Strengths	1	2	3	4	5	1	2	3	4	5	
1 Bank network	++	++	++			++	++				10
2 Service quality	+	-	++			+	++				5
3 Lending power	++	O	O			+	++				5
4											
5											
	2	-2	3			1	3				7
Weaknesses											Threats
1 Systems capability	-	=	O			=	-				-6
2 Geographic organization	=	=	-			-	=				-7
3											
4											
5											

Future Opportunities:
1 Project finance
2 Global cash management
3 Global HNWI banking
4
5

Future Threats:
1 Foreign bank threats
2 Non-bank competition
3
4
5

Figure 2.7 Bank SWOT analysis

weaknesses to a limited number, executives are forced to qualitatively prioritize their thoughts. A number of issues will emerge strongly from the exercise as being especially important. This is achieved by listing all the issues identified and subsequently distilling them in open discussion to the overall most important.

Key market opportunities
Identification of the key market opportunities suggests the strategic direction for the bank. Comparison of the cross-impact scores with the bank's identified strengths and weaknesses suggests how these opportunities might be realized and what internal weaknesses need to be corrected.

Key market threats
Identification of key threats should lead to a focusing on counterstrategies to offset the effects of these threats.

Internal communications
A detailed and common understanding of the position of the bank is an important ingredient in getting organizational acceptance of overall strategy. Compare the key issues developed at various levels of management. When these are relatively similar, the organization is viewing the internal and external environment in a like manner. When a large divergence occurs it is an indication that a communication gap exists which needs correction.

Management cohesion
At each level of management, and especially at senior levels, check the total number of different issues identified. Where the responses indicate a wide variation in issues, this implies a lack of cohesion in the way management sees the organization and its external environment. A cohesive management group by comparison will identify a substantial number of common issues.

Relative field forces
Sum the pluses and minuses in each direction. A bank with more weaknesses than strengths will tend to have an overall greater negative score than positive. Similarly, a bank facing more threats than opportunities will also tend to have more negative than positives. Check also for the particular strengths and weaknesses, threats and opportunities which emerge as the strongest negatives or positives as an indication of their relative importance for management action.

Having completed the SWOT analysis, check the outcome against the bank's present strategy. It is common to find that existing plans fail to address many of the key strategic issues identified. Check therefore:

- Does the existing plan deal adequately with all the strategic issues?
- Does the analysis suggest any change in short-term strategy?
- Does the analysis suggest any change in long-term strategy?
- Are any communications programs necessary to achieve organizational understanding?
- Does top management need to improve its cohesion?
- Are any particular units of the organization in need of reinforcement as a priority?

2.3.8 Competitive Position Measures

In addition to an overall status assessment, it is important to review your bank's position in each of the markets in which it is operating or plans to operate. The following items are important measures of competitive strength. Where 'relative' is used the measure is an assessment of your bank relative to its three largest competitors. In addition, it is important to identify any 'key success factors' which it is essential to be good at in competing in a particular market.

Competitive Position Measures

- Absolute market share: Measured as your market share of the defined served market.
- Relative share: Measured as your share as a percentage of that of the combined share of your three largest competitors.
- Trend in market share: The trend in your market share over the past three years.
- Relative profitability: The relative profitability of your business as a percentage of the average of your three largest competitors.
- Relative service quality: An assessment of the relative level of the quality of your service compared with that of your three largest competitors from the *customer* point of view.
- Relative price: The relative price of your service as a percentage of the average of your three largest competitors.
- Customer concentration: The number of customers making up 80 per cent of your business. Few customers may increase your vulnerabilty to customer pressure.
- Rate of service innovation: The percentage of sales from products introduced in the past three years indicates the maturity of your services.
- Relative capital intensity: The capital intensity of your business as a percentage of that of your three largest competitors. A higher capital intensity is usually a weakness.

Competitive Position

From the competitive position measures assess the bank's relative strength. Score each factor from 1 to 5, with the high score representing a very strong competitive position and the low score a very weak one. Sum the position scores for each factor and calculate the overall percentage of the total possible score. This figure can be used to plot your competitive position on the market portfolio matrix. You can also weight the relative importance of each of the factors according to the consensus opinion of your managers. In general, market share, relative share, capital intensity and product quality are usually especially important factors.

Key Success Factors

Using the form shown in Figure 2.8, indicate the relative importance of each of the key success factors in achieving success in each market and the relative strength or weakness of your bank in each factor. This will give some indication of likely strategic priorities and provide a valuable input in assessing the practicality of attacking particular market segments.

Capability	Level of Importance					Your Strength or Weakness				
	Low 1				High 5	Low 1				High 5
Selling										
Network										
Operations										
Financing										
Innovation										
Systems										
Promotion/ communications										
Other (specify)										

Figure 2.8   Key success factor analysis

2.3.9 Measuring Market Attractiveness

Next, from the data on market/industry characteristics, assess the relative attractiveness of each of the markets in which the bank is engaged. The following characteristics are useful in assessing market attractiveness. In addition, examine those other characteristics which may suggest appropriate strategies for each market.

Market Attractiveness Measures

- Size: The size of a market is important, and obtaining a reasonable share should represent a sufficient volume of the bank's business to make it worthwhile to provide the service.

- Past growth rate: Examine the past growth rate as a guide to assessing the future trends.
- Projected growth rate: Indicate your base case assumption about future growth prospects. Sensitivity analysis later might review other possible rates of growth.
- Number of competitors: Indicate the number of competitors in the market. The larger the number the less attractive the market.
- Competitor concentration: Identify the number of competitors accounting for 80 per cent of the market. More concentrated markets are generally more attractive, fragmented markets are usually more price-competitive.
- Market profitability: Specify the average level of profitability for the market.
- Degree of product differentiation: Indicate what percentage of services in the market are differentiated. The higher the level of differentiation the more attractive the market, since high differentiation reduces the level of price competition.
- Level of capital intensity: Indicate the level of capital intensity of the market.
- High capital intensity markets are less attractive as they have a lower rate of return on assets.
- Relative customer power: Indicate the relative strength of customers *versus* the banks. Usually a small number of large customers means high relative customer power.
- Profitability trend: Indicate the trend in market profitability.
- Market fit: Assess the fit of this market relative to the overall position of the bank.

Market attractiveness

For each factor score the market on a scale from 1 to 5, with the high score indicating a high level of attractiveness and the low score indicating the market as unattractive. Sum the scores to arrive at the overall score out of a possible maximum. This figure can be used to plot the position of the market on the attractiveness dimension of the market portfolio matrix. You can also weight the relative importance of each of the factors according to the consensus opinion of your managers. In general, market size, growth rate, capital intensity, customer concentration and market fit are usually especially important factors.

Strategy Characteristics

Certain market/industry characteristics are useful in assessing effective strategies. Such characteristics include:

- Importance of the service to the customer: Essential services tend to be less subject to price erosion, involve more critical buying decisions, and are likely to enjoy higher customer loyalty.

- Purchase frequency: Low purchase frequency services may be more difficult to penetrate but less price-sensitive since customer awareness will be lower.
- Customer concentration: High customer concentration usually increases customer bargaining power but makes it easier to change market share by gaining relative few new accounts.
- Market saturation: Selling to new or potential users is usually different to selling to established purchasers.
- Barriers to entry: High barriers to entry favor established suppliers. Low barriers encourage intensive competition.
- Barriers to exit: High barriers to exit encourage intensive competition, especially in slow growth markets.

2.3.10 Environmental Factors

The assessment of market/industry characteristics or competitive position is based on assumptions about the general economic and social environment which may be critical to its validity. Moreover, changes in the external environment can affect the desirability of the potential strategies that can be adopted to change the relative position in the market. These environmental assumptions should be made explicit, and if there is a reasonable probability that an external change would have a major impact on a proposed strategy its effect should be assessed and the sensitivity identified.

Check your assessment of market/industry characteristics and competitive position against key environmental factors. These should include consideration of the following and the results should be set out on a form such as that shown in Figure 2.9.

Trends in economic conditions
National/regional GNP
National inflation
Foreign exchange rates
Interest rates
Unemployment levels
Money supply
Industry structure

Trends in demographics
Birth rate
Population size
Age distribution
Socioeconomic distribution
Geographic population distribution
Education/skill distribution

Key factor	Factor impact on SBU strategy	Expected factor change in next 5 years and timing	Possible strategic reaction
Economic			
Demographic			
Socio-cultural			
Technological			
Political/legal			

Figure 2.9   Macro economic environmental analysis

Socio-cultural trends
Lifestyle trends
Career expectations
Education trends
Public opinion
Family formation rate
Banking usage trends

Trends in technology
Industry technology changes
Non-bank competitor investment
EFT systems
Information processing systems
Machine banking

Political/Legal trends
Bank regulations
Tax laws
Exchange controls
Attitudes to foreign banks
Attitudes to non-bank competitors

2.3.11 Strategic Market Portfolio Development

The relative positions of each of the bank's business activities need to be identified next, using the competitive position/market attractiveness matrix illustrated in Figure 2.10. Each cell on the matrix suggests an alternative investment strategy for the business contained in it as shown. Businesses in the top left-hand corner are high in market attractiveness and have a strong competitive position. Such businesses still enjoy high growth and should receive priority for any investment support needed. Businesses in the grow/penetrate cell are also primary candidates for investment in an effort to improve competitive position while growth prospects remain high. Defend/ invest position businesses are in less attractive markets but investment should be maintained as needed to defend the strong competitive position established. Businesses in the bottom left corner are candidates for harvesting. The market attractiveness is low, indicating probably that the growth is low but the relative competitive position remains high. Such businesses are therefore usually producing good profits which cannot justifiably be reinvested back. Surplus cash flow is therefore withdrawn for redistribution to other businesses requiring investment funds.

Businesses in the center are candidates for selective investment, usually where refined segmentation options are available. Businesses at the bottom center and right center are candidates for withdrawal/divestment or for

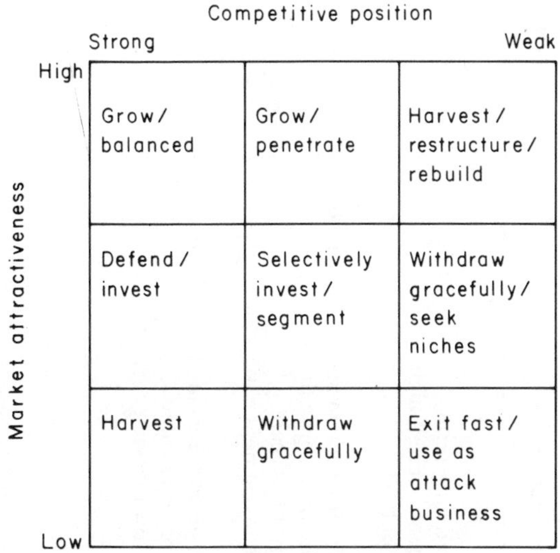

Competitive position

	Strong		Weak
High	Grow/ balanced	Grow/ penetrate	Harvest / restructure/ rebuild
	Defend / invest	Selectively invest / segment	Withdraw gracefully/ seek niches
Low	Harvest	Withdraw gracefully	Exit fast / use as attack business

(Market attractiveness — vertical axis label, High to Low)

Figure 2.10 Bank strategic market portfolio

seeking small niches, for example in certain geographic markets, where useful profits can be achieved. Businesses in the bottom right cell are both in unattractive markets and have a weak competitive position. Such businesses may be losing money and will not be likely to produce a strong positive cash flow. As a result they should be considered for divestment or closure. A more sophisticated alternative might be to use them as attack businesses to be deployed against a competitor's harvest businesses to depress their cash-generating capability. Detailed alternative market segment investment strategies are shown in Figure 2.11. Although the listed investment strategies can conceivably be used with any attractiveness/position combination the choice should be guided by the cost and probability of success in moving from the existing to the desired position. An ideal portfolio resembles that illustrated in Figure 2.12.

After the bank's portfolio has been mapped, each market should be assigned a specific investment strategy and an associated objective which indicates the desired results in the market segment. Examples of such objectives might include:

Market A: Grow/penetrate
Enter Middle East high net worth individual market in 1981 and achieve share of 1 per cent by 1984 to obtain deposits of $1bn and net revenue of $10m.

Market B: Harvest
Improve ROA to 0.6 per cent after tax by 1983 by giving up customers with high servicing costs and reduce net assets exposed by $250m in Belgium.

Category	Assessment of contribution to earnings	General objective	Investment commitment	Willing to accept		
				Payout	Near Term vol.	Term Impact ROI
I Grow/penetrate	Significant increment to earnings in long run	Penetrate market to establish strong future position	Sustained long-term investment. Accept high investment risk	Long	←	→
II Grow/balanced	Significant current *and* long-term earnings growth	Maintain current strong position in growth market with little or no reduction in ROI	Sustained investment at rate to maintain growth with market. Accept medium investment risk	Short to med.	←	↑
III Selectively invest	Significant current and future earnings but limited growth with stable margins	Maintain or improve ROI as primary objective. Exploit selective opportunities for volume growth if available	Limited investments in targets or opportunity. Accept low investment risk	Short	↑	↑
IV Defend	Significant current earnings. Declining margin. Limited volume growth	Defend earnings base until attractive opportunities can replace	Invest only in response to competitive inroads. Accept medium investment risk.	Short	↑	→

V Harvest	Significant current earnings from strong position but outlook for flat or declining market	Maximize current earnings. Allow gradual erosion in share if it improves margin	Disinvest gradually at rate to avoid collapse of business	
VI Restructure/ rebuild	Opportunity for at least a one-time increment in earnings where market share at least average	Eliminate current deficiencies to restore profitability	One-time investment dictated by nature of deficiencies. Accept medium investment risk	Short
VII Withdraw	Declining market and earnings. Possible one-time earnings. Increment from sale or elimination of loss	Withdraw from market on most favorable terms	Disinvest	
VIII Hold	Nature of opportunity not established	Carry out strategy development while maintaining *status quo*	No investment until strategy developed. Commit to resources required for strategy development	

Figure 2.11   Alternative market investment strategies

40

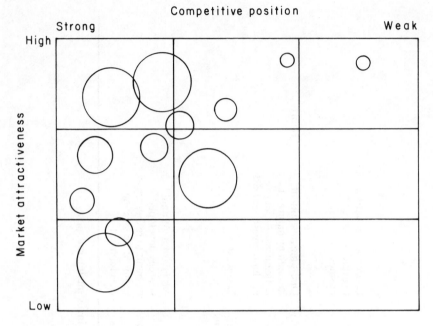

Figure 2.12   Ideal market portfolio

2.3.12 Market Segment Plan Development

The achievement of the portfolio investment strategy objective usually requires the manager of the operational unit involved to make strategic changes in key variables under his control. The change in each key variable is established as a unit objective and an action plan is developed for the achievement of this. The bringing together of the plans to achieve the overall investment strategy forms the unit strategy.

In developing action plans bear in mind that any changes should be strategic in nature and within the control of the unit manager concerned. The variables on which a manager can usually operate are as follows:

1. *Market segmentation.* Redefinition of existing market segments can form the basis for improved marketing differentiation; e.g. attack the financial services segment of the international corporate market.
2. *Change served market boundary;* e.g. enlarge geographic coverage of served market for international cash management services.
3. *Change breadth or mix of product/service range;* e.g. introduce multicurrency international cash management services.
4. *Change rate of new/improved product introduction;* e.g. introduce 'smart' terminals for corporate treasurers as part of new cash management service.

5. *Change quality of products;* e.g. reduce transaction error rate by 20 per cent.
6. *Change pricing;* e.g. reduce prices for international clearances by using automated systems.
7. *Change method or level of selling;* e.g. retrain account officers to offer leasing products.
8. *Change method or scope of distribution;* e.g. open regional branches with on-line FX facilities.
9. *Change level of productivity;* e.g. introduce automated back office systems to reduce staffing by 15 per cent.
10. *Change capacity;* e.g. introduce new computer systems to increase transaction capacity by 30 per cent.

The unit strategic plan therefore mirrors the corporate and divisional plans and comprises:

1. *Mission statement.* This reflects the scope of activities and strategy assigned to the unit in developing its specific market segment or segments. The statement should be consistent with that of the division and bank as a whole. It should also identify the product and customer parameters of the segment and the relationship between the unit and others of the bank.
2. *Objectives.* These should be quantified for the overall unit and provide measurable parameters for the unit mission. The long-range objectives should address financial and strategic outcomes such as level of return on assets, profits, growth rate and market share.
3. *Assumptions.* These should be identified for the specific market segment and cover environmental change, competitive activity, service requirements and future market expectations.
4. *Competitive strength.* The position of key competitors for the specific market segment should be assessed including their market shares and relative strengths and weaknesses. Note that specific competitors at the market segment level may differ from the competitors which pose a serious overall threat at divisional and corporate level. Thus in many local markets major competitors will be indigenous banks whereas overall corporate threats may be posed by major international banks.
5. *Market opportunity.* This is assessed at all levels of the bank but the specific expectations are again spelt out at the market segment level.
6. *Investment strategy.* This identifies the specific investment priority expected for this segment.
7. *Strategic variable change.* Identifies the action plans required to achieve the desired change in strategic variables for this unit.
8. *Implementation programs.* These set out the specific programs whereby each action plan achieves its goals. They include a beginning

and an end date, specific objectives, strategic milestones in development and detailed resource needs.

9. *Expected financial results.* Identifies the specific financial outcomes which can be expected of the unit given its stratgy.

2.3.13 Action Plan Development

Action plans will each consist of one or more programs designed to change the methods, process, staffing levels, organizational skills, equipment, systems or premises of the bank unit. In addition each will specify the resources needed to carry them out, covering such areas as funding, capital, country limits, systems, equipment and personnel. An example of the hierarchy of action plans and programs is given below:

Market segment: Multinational wholesale banking .
Market portfolio strategy: selective investment.
Objective: To improve ROA from existing average level of 0.5 per cent to 0.7 per cent level with no more than a 2 per cent loss of market share. With market share at 9 per cent and expected market growth at 4 per cent, earnings are expected to increase at 7 per cent in real terms over the next three years.
Management strategy: Initiate an increased pricing policy based on actual services delivered, selectively change market coverage to delete those accounts producing an inadequate return, improve overall service quality and differentiation capability and increase processing productivity by introducing advanced systems.

Action plan 1: increase pricing
Objective: Increase pricing to ensure an average ROA of 0.7 per cent but not more than the price leader in the market.

Program 1: Establish account/product cost measurement system.
Objective: Create a cost measurement and reporting system capable of providing cost by service by customer on a monthly basis.
Timing: Program commencement August 1983, completion by December 1984.
Method: Unit task force with support from cashiers, corporate planning and systems. Design of standardized format by November 1983; manual trial of format by February 1984 for 100 leading accounts; test of computer systems February 1984; data collection of top 250 accounts by July 1984; system trials August–October 1984; system introduction November 1984; review and finalization December 1984.
Estimated cost/benefit: Total cost for this program estimated at $280,000, made up of:

      Additional personnel costs $80,000

Systems development	$110,000
Equipment	$60,000
Other	$20,000
Expected benefits	$280,000
Non-profitable account	$500,000
Elimination	

Organization: Task force chairmanship and program.

Responsibility: Manager, J. R. Shapiro.

Resources: Personnel Unit staff are available; additional staffing resources required include:

Operations, 2 systems engineers part-time for 1½ years.

Cashiers, 1 cost accountant part-time for 1½ years.

Corporate planning, information systems design section input for ensuring consistency with bank MIPAC design.

Systems

New systems development required linked to existing account statements.

Equipment

Existing IBM mainframe will be used as primary data base.

Additional linked micronetwork for account officers' unit management on-line account interrogation system.

Funding

No additional funding required.

Program 2: Introduce account-based planning system.
Objective: Introduce an account-based planning system which provides profitability budgets by account by service line on a quarterly basis by December 1983 for key accounts.

Program 3: Plan pricing change process.
Objective: Provide pricing schedules timing by account type for account officer usage prior to changes. Prepare contingency plans in case market share impact exceeds expectations.

The additional programs would also be broken down in detail, with objectives, timing, method, cost/benefit expectations, milestones, organization and responsibilty and resource needs. Similarly, action plans would be prepared for market coverage change, product quality, product range and productivity, each of which would also be subdivided into detailed implementation programs. Note the strategic milestones used to monitor progress against the implementation programs do not cover financial variables since these options usually lag the strategic changes and are unsuitable as measures. However, at the program level it is usually possible to develop fairly realistic preliminary cost/benefit estimates which in turn should be reflected in their impact on key financial variables.

2.3.14 Divisional and Departmental Strategic Planning

At the divisional or departmental level strategy is usually determined for more than one market segment. As a consequence a division like the bank as a whole may be required to operate a set or portfolio of strategies for its markets. Thus the division management may need to develop action plans to achieve its market mix objectives which are different and distinctive from the market segment action plans. These overall action plans may often address the following variables:

1. *Management effectiveness.* Typically, programs might address division organization structure, management information systems, management training and rewards and sanction systems.
2. *Operations/administrative efficiency.* Programs in this area might involve creating or eliminating central processing activities, changing shared services, or introducing new automated systems which span a number of market segments or divisions.
3. *Innovation.* Programs here would cover strategy development, new market segment identification and service development capability.
4. *Resource procurement.* Typical programs might cover reduction or addition of personnel, funding, premises and equipment at the overall divisional level.

Care must be taken in distinguishing between divisional and unit plans to ensure that as much focus as possible is directed on the purpose of each program so that its link to strategic objectives can be clearly identified and measured. The use of overall divisional action plans should therefore be carefully scrutinized to ensure they do not become dumping grounds. This concept of divisional action plan can also be extended to those at the overall bank level to form a hierarchy of plans each level of which supports that above it. The plan hierarchy at the market segment end is illustrated in Figure 2.13.

Summary

The process of bank strategic planning is a vital ingredient in the development of systematic strategic management at all levels of the bank. The plan itself should be developed to become an important working document for management and not produced once a year as a chore and never used again. However, it is only a guide and framework for action; it is not and never can be a substitute for initiative, drive and creativity, which can only be supplied by the manager and his officers.

2.4 STRATEGY TESTING

The market plan review presents an opportunity to evaluate the strategy chosen for a particular market. It also helps to provide a feedback to market

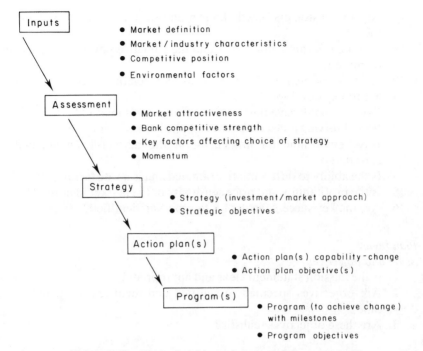

Figure 2.13   Bank plan hierarchy, market segment level

segment managers and give additional insights into the thinking behind the development of unit strategy. Use the following checklist as a guide to the review and for focusing upon items to be discussed in greater depth. In particular, check for inconsistencies in the plan. This meeting, however, should be seen as a constructive opportunity for two-way feedback and communication and not as an interrogation of unit management plans, opening the way to destructive criticism.

Strategic market plan evaluation

Market evaluation
1. Are the data sufficient to make an adequate evaluation of the market?
2. If not, what additional data are required and where should they be obtained?
3. Is the served market clearly defined?
4. What is the size of the market in terms of volume and value?
5. What is the historic growth rate and future projection?
6. How many customers are involved? How many account for 50 and 80 per cent of volume?
7. Is the decision process of these accounts known and can the bank reach and influence the decision process?

8. Are the customers' needs known and do the banks' services meet these?
9. Are the relevant competitors and their relative power and strategies identified?
10. Is the assessment of the bank's position relative to the competitors accurately developed?
11. Does the bank have the resources to serve this market?
12. Would serving it be consistent with the bank's overall objectives?
13. Have environmental influences on the market been adequately considered?
14. Is the ability to differentiate examined and is it satisfactory?
15. Is the profitability and price sensitivity of the market identified?
16. Are the key success factors for this market identified?

Plan review
Mission and objectives
1. Is the mission statement clear and appropriate?
2. Are objectives specified, quantified and identified by people and time?
3. Are these objectives realistic?

Environment and market assumptions
4. Have all important assumptions been identified and taken into consideration?
5. Are the assumptions reasonable?
6. What is the basis of information behind the assumptions?

Competitive strength
7. Is the bank's market share and those of the major competitors clearly identified?
8. Is the bank's profitability relative to competition identified?
9. Is the bank's relative service quality identified and evaluated?
10. Is the price of the bank's service evaluated relative to major competitors?
11. Is the bank's delivery system and marketing effort identified relative to major competitors?
12. Is the bank's level of resources committed relative to major competitors identified and evaluated?

Opportunity assessment
13. Are the opportunities clearly defined and assessed as to direction and potential impact?

14. Are any external threats clearly identified and assessed as to direction and potential impact?

Market segment portfolio strategy
15. Is the market segment portfolio strategy of each business clearly established?
16. Is the strategy proposed consistent with the market portfolio strategy position?

Action plan objectives
17. Are the action plan objectives clearly identified and quantified for each strategic factor in terms of the level and nature of change planned?
18. Does each subprogram have its expected objective specified in terms of its contribution to the desired change in the relevant strategic factor?
19. Are the attack plan objectives supportive and consistent with the market strategy and market segment objective?
20. Is the action plan objective consistent with the inputs and assessments, including anticipated competitor responses?

Program plans
21. Are the steps required to implement the programs clearly identified together with appropriate milestones?
22. Are the necessary staffing levels needed identified within the unit?
23. Is the necessary skill mix needed identified within the unit?
24. Are any training and/or recruitment procedures identified?
25. Are the personnel/staffing skills needed from elsewhere in the bank identified?
26. Are the communications/organizational linkages between the unit and other parts of the bank identified?
27. Are the funding resources needed identified? Are they costed?
28. Are the credit procedures and risks identified?
29. Are any systems/operations requirements identified and costed?
30. Are any equipment requirements identified and costed?
31. Are the potential competitor reactions identified?
32. Has 'what if' analysis been conducted to assess the impact of changes?
33. Have contingency plans been developed?
34. Have the cost/benefit estimates been prepared and are they reasonable?
35. Has the organization for each program been spelt out together with the identification of the individual responsible?

36. Does the program seem feasible in the light of resource availability, past experience and unit capabilities?
37. Will the accomplishment of the program achieve the program objective?
38. Will the accomplishment of all the programs in each action plan achieve the action plan objective?

CHAPTER 3

Implementing Strategic Planning Successfully

3.1 INTRODUCTION

There is no one right way to plan in any organization. The methodology proposed in this book works in banks but the ideal system for any bank is likely to be an adaptation that fits its own particular strategy, structure, values and internal culture. As a general rule, however, bankers have not traditionally been good at strategic planning and may still have strong reservations about its value to them and their banks. While this attitude is now breaking down, there is no doubt that in order for the strategic management and marketing skills introduced within the industry to have a better chance of successful implementation certain conditions need to be present. This chapter examines these requirements and provides a checklist to enable you to evaluate your existing strategic planning system and check that it is working and that it adequately meets the needs of the bank.

3.2 CONDITIONS FOR SUCCESSFUL IMPLEMENTATION

3.2.1 A Recognized Need

For strategic planning to be fully accepted within a bank there must be a clear and unequivocal recognized need that increased attention should be paid to the forward direction of the bank. Normally such a need is first recognized by groups within the bank, especially those under pressure. It is not always recognized by the bank's leadership until it is too late for the leader currently in power. Need recognition thus usually comes about through the emergence of the following factors:

Unsatisfactory Financial Performance

When financial performance has deteriorated in relative terms by comparison with major competitors top management will come under increasing pressure from large shareholders, and especially institutions, to reestablish their relative market position. For example, the relative decline of Chase Manhattan compared with Citibank in the mid-1970s eventually prompted the board to introduce strategic planning by bringing in expertise from the US General Electric Company.

Successful Competitive Pressures

The superior performance of key competitors often prompts a management reaction in the form of the introduction of strategic plans to counter the competitor's strategy. This phenomenon is especially likely when rivalries are seen as being particularly close. For example, the apparent success of Continental Illinois over its close rival First of Chicago was to lead the latter's board to bring in a new chief executive with the specific task of introducing strategic planning to counter this success.

Sudden and Unplanned Serious Loss

When sudden and unplanned losses occur there is always a major inquest inside any bank. The result of such an inquest usually means changes in control systems in an attempt to prevent any recurrence of the problem; reorganization to penalize those responsible for the area of loss; and reappraisal of the planning system to try to reduce business uncertainty. Thus the failure of Chase Manhattan at Drysdale and Penn Square has resulted in a review of control systems and reorganization of the sector concerned.

Strategic Shock

A strategic shock takes place when a major unexpected event occurs for which top management has no prepared response. This could be an unexpected and unwelcome acquisition bid or tender offer. If management has not adequately planned for the future the shock of such an event forces rapid and rigorous reappraisal of plans and the planning system.

Without the presence of such a recognized need by those with the power to ensure that planning system change should take place, it is unlikely that it will. Indeed in banks where strategic planning is not well established its introduction is likely to be strongly resisted, especially within line banking units, since it threatens the existing power structure and provides a potential check on perhaps previously unmonitored and essentially uncontrolled autonomy.

3.2.2 Leadership Commitment

Without the clear commitment of the chief executive officer planning is unlikely to be successful, since planners will lack the necessary political muscle to gain line management commitment. This does not mean that the planning unit itself should be overpowerful but rather that it should be acting as the arm of senior executive management in the construction and implementation of bank strategic plans. Moreover, if senior management is not seen to take the planning process seriously it will lack credibility within the bank.

In practice the introduction of planning, and certainly significant changes in the system of planning, usually takes place shortly after a change in the chairmanship or chief executive officer of the bank. In part the change in planning may be seen as an element of the new chief executive's method of adjusting the culture of the bank to take on new strategic directions. Examples of this type of shift where the strategic planning system becomes a more important element in the management of the bank include the appointment of Barry Sullivan as chairman at First Chicago and that of Sam Armacost to the presidency of Bank of America.

3.2.3 External Catalyst

Most of the major changes in bank strategic planning systems that have occurred in leading banks to date have been undertaken in conjunction with the use of external catalysts, mainly management consultants. This is perhaps not altogether surprising for two main reasons.

Firstly, if the bank had the internal skills to introduce the strategic planning system itself then it would probably already have done so. However, banks have not long been concerned with the industrial concepts of strategic management and few line bankers have been trained in an understanding of them. Therefore it is perhaps natural to turn to external consultants as a source of assistance and conceptual advice. Unfortunately, few consultants have used their conceptual tools within the banking industry and as a result a number of major contracts have been conducted to introduce strategic change in banks where the consultants have spent much of their time learning about the banking industry and trying to modify their concepts to fit its needs.

Secondly, consultants are often used by incoming chief executives as an element in modifying the power base and culture of the organization. One essential ingredient in achieving such a change is the introduction of management information, planning and control systems suited to this purpose.

3.2.4 Suitable Reorganization

The introduction of a suitable strategic planning system potentially provides a significant new tool for the management of the bank as a whole. A carefully developed strategy will normally subdivide the bank's business into a portfolio of opportunities with alternative investment strategies. This concept, once established, has an important impact on the way the bank is organized. Structure will be adapted to fit the needs of strategy rather than, as is common, the strategy being unsatisfactorily fitted on to the existing structure.

With the introduction of strategic planning top management has a substantially improved knowledge of the bank's businesses and can delegate authority with more confidence. The flow of information and the manner of central management intervention will, however, be changed. In practice this shift in organization very often forms a further element in the succession strategy of a new chief executive officer.

While the structure of the bank should fit its strategy appropriately, successful planning will usually require the creation of a separate planning unit which is concerned with the bank as a whole. Planning also takes place in the line divisions, but the central unit should be perceived as an arm of the board and in particular the chief executive officer. It is also important for strategic as distinct from financial planning that such a unit should not form part of the finance department or treasury. However, it is desirable that planning and control should be separated, the controller's function being that of plan monitoring, utilizing control systems in whose design the planning unit is concerned. The controller's function in this respect is not that of the bank audit unit, and it is noticeable that some banks have found it desirable to create a new management information systems unit.

3.2.5 Development of an Information Base

A key problem in initiating a strategic planning system is the lack of availability of suitable data for strategic analysis. This is ironic in that, as organizations, banks contain more data than most about the transactions they conduct. Unfortunately, however, these data are not usually organized to produce information suitable for management purposes. Further, banks do not collect some information of particular value to the strategic planner such as market share, systematic competitive intelligence, and the like.

As a consequence, one of the first prerequisites for successfully introducing strategic planning is the collection and organizing of suitable data for strategic analysis. Typical information required would include data to allow for:

— Correct market identification
— Market segmentation
— Market attractiveness measurement
— Competitive position measurement
— Business/customer/product profitability analysis
— Strategic resource requirements assessment (human, systems and financial)
— Control system design
— Reward system development
— Organizational change

The development of an integrated data base for management information purposes is a critical ingredient in developing bank marketing strategy. Very few banks have to date introduced such data bases because to do so takes a considerable period of time and expense and requires the transformation of basic transaction accounting procedures. However, without such a data base it is not normally possible for the bank to plan accurate segmentation of either retail or corporate accounts. In practice the introduction of an integrated data base usually also means a specific segregation of corporate and retail business because the data needs for each customer base are normally significantly different. Moreover, such segregation permits different service offerings to be efficiently made to each major customer class.

3.2.6 Suitable Control System Design

Without adequate monitoring of progress towards strategic goals it is impossible to tell whether planned strategies are succeeding or not. By and large the development of control systems in banks has not been strong. In part this is due to difficulties of measurement, However, it is also substantially due to management neglect. For example, many banks claim it is extremely difficult if not impossible to assess adequately the costs of individual services. It is true that shared costs are common in banking, making precise measurement more difficult. But for strategic purposes it is possible, with adequate management, to generate an approximate cost structure with only limited effort. A more detailed discussion of service costing is made in Chapter 8.

As shown in Figure 3.1, however, the components of bank control systems vary widely in their quality and in most banks strategic controls do not exist at all. Most branch-based banks have relatively good measures of profitability by

Control system component	Qualitative assessment		
	Report availability	Report clarity	Concept validity
Profit measurement			
Branches/departments	Very good	Fair	Fair
Services	Fair	Fair	Poor
Accounts	Poor	Poor	Poor
Funds management	Very poor	Very poor	Very poor
Risk measurement			
Credit risk	Very good	Good	Good
Interest rate risk	Poor	Poor	Very poor
Exchange rate risk	Fair	Poor	Very poor

Figure 3.1　Qualitative assessment of bank control systems

branch, although this can be influenced by the internal pool rate for funds. In the main, however, controls are satisfactory. Control systems which provide adequate information on either individual services or customers are much less well developed. Few banks have to date developed worldwide controls for large accounts like those referred to in Chapter 6. Similarly, with a few exceptions such as foreign exchange execution and other major services, few banks have developed satisfactory controls over individual non-interest fee-based products.

The development of an appropriate management information and control system allows the bank to better decide on segmentation, delivery system, market communication and pricing strategies. Without such information, for much of the time the bank may be providing uneconomic services, to customer groups which may be unattractive, through an inappropriate and overexpensive delivery system. Further, marketing and advertising may be devoted to exacerbating the difficulties. While profitable services and customers thus exist within a bank, without adequate management information the bank does not know which of its customers and services these are. At the same time, the bank cannot measure its progress towards the achievement of strategic objectives since these cannot really be set without some way of measuring them.

The assessment of risk is similarly weak in some areas. While banks have long been concerned with credit analysis, the 'lemming syndrome' reappears regularly every few years when heavy losses occur as a result of individual banks rushing into a fashionable marketplace and in so doing abandoning all their normal credit assessment procedures. In the mid-1970s this occurred in property, in the late 1970s in shipping, and in the early 1980s in sovereign risk lending and some areas of energy and project finance.

The precise choice of what controls to concentrate on will vary for individual banks depending upon the primary strategy. This is illustrated in Figure 3.2 for banks with different emphases in their core strategy. Bank A is primarily a bank with multiple branches servicing retail and small business customers. The bank has a lesser emphasis on servicing large corporate accounts, in investment management and in related banking services such as credit finance and leasing. The control system priority for Bank A is to gain a clear understanding of profitability by branch and secondly, to evaluate the profitability of the individual services offered. Customer-based controls are of less significance, while extensive funds management and detailed key account controls are not required. Similarly, the priority risk assessment in Bank A relates to credit assessment, while exchange rate risk is of less significance since the bank's customer base is likely to be localized.

By contrast, Bank B is primarily a corporate bank with only a limited retail activity, usually within a limited geographic environment by comparison with the large account needs which may well be international. The control priority in such a bank is for an account-based profit system, with branch-based profits

Control system priorities

Risk measurement

	Credit	Interest rate	Exchange rate
	1	2	3
	2	1	3
	3	1	2

Profit measurement

	Branches	Services	Key accounts	Non-key accounts	Funds mgt.
	1	2	▨	3	▨
	2	3	1	4	▨
	4	3	2	▨	1

% profit breakdown

Retail & small corporate banking

Large corporate banking

Investment management

Related banking services

Bank A

Bank B

Bank C

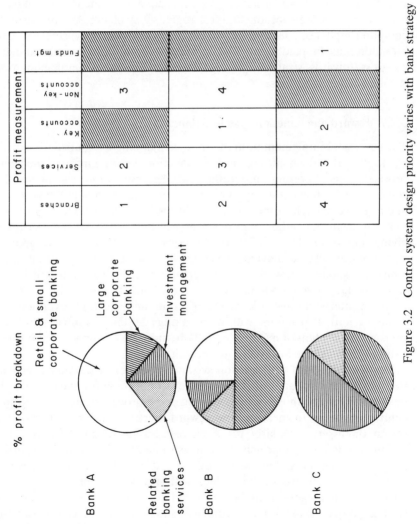

Figure 3.2 Control system design priority varies with bank strategy

second and profits by service line third. Similarly, the primary risk for such a bank is interest rate variation, with credit assessment second and exchange rate variation third.

In addition to these formal financial controls, however, banks also need strategic controls to monitor the progress of strategic plans and point to contingency action as appropriate at specific predetermined trigger points. Unlike financial controls, strategic controls require not only the analysis of internal factors but also external market characteristics such as market share change, relative cost, relative product quality, relative market coverage, and the like. Further, the data are future oriented, whereas financial control tends to monitor historic performance. As a consequence strategic control data are less accurate, more sporadic and less regularly available, less processable by computer and less susceptible to variance analysis. Nevertheless, careful attention must be paid to introducing suitable monitoring systems to measure progress towards strategic plan goals based upon the implementation of detailed action programs.

3.2.7 Reward and Sanction System Balance

The successful implementation of strategic planning is significantly enhanced by ensuring that the bank's reward and sanction system reinforces the planning process. It is therefore important that the motivation system should be consistent with bank strategy, with behavior positive to plan being rewarded and negative behavior sanctioned. Traditionally banks have tended to reward more on seniority rather than performance but a growing number are now giving significant levels of variable reward which are based upon plan performance. Plan achievement should thus be seen as important and line managers should know that their performance against plan will be taken seriously. Dependent upon the culture of the bank, this may require the taking up of an interventionist role by the planning unit. Such intervention can be positive in that planners will work alongside line banking units in the preparation of plans or negative in that pressure can be applied to improve line plans or to intervene in cases of non-performance.

In aligning reward and sanction systems, however, it should be recognized that the same standards of performance do not apply to each area of bank business. Thus for those businesses assigned a growth strategy, the principal control might be to measure and reward market share growth rather than return on assets. Similarly for a harvest business, maximization of cash resources might be the principal for measurement and reward. One particular problem which must be recognized is that the achievement of strategic objectives cannot usually take place within a short-term time frame. This means that managers must be rewarded for endeavoring to achieve such strategic objectives and undue emphasis should not be placed on short-term performance goals in the reward and sanction system. Unfortunately, all too many banks force executives to focus on short-term, one-year operating budget performance and so neglect the longer-term strategic perspective.

3.2.8 Good Communications

It is imperative for successful strategic planning to communicate the desires of top management and the aspirations held about individual business units. Banks lacking leadership which does not adequately communicate its intentions will find that there is inconsistency in the strategic objectives of individual bank units and the bank as a whole. Communication also aids in creating a commonality of purpose, helps to overcome the ultimate inertia that tends to exist in most organizations and acts as a positive motivating force. Finally, communication is necessary in isolating and reducing any potential resistance.

There are a number of ways that good communication can be achieved:

— Most important, clear and positive leadership is required. The caliber of the leadership of an organization can make a disproportionate difference to the way in which the structure functions.

— In addition to providing leadership itself, the leadership of the bank should adopt a well-communicated and easy to understand corporate mission. Often a superordinate goal can be helpful in this respect, providing it is believable, relevant and demanding in terms of the task that needs to be fulfilled in order to achieve it.

— 'Indoctrination' programs to introduce participants to the corporate culture can be an important ingredient in establishing strategic plan goals. J. P. Morgan, for example, brings all its executives to the bank in New York for a period of initial training which in the main is concerned with introducing them to the culture and norms of the bank.

— An initial approach to introducing strategic planning after commitment by top management is to gradually broaden the initial group to create a 'central values' group of top management. This central values group can then be expanded to ensure a growing cadre of executives who identify with the planning system and strategy adopted by the bank.

— A similar method of breaking down potential line unit resistance is the creation of cross-organizational task forces designed to address specific strategic issues identified as being important for the future of the bank.

— Finally, the basic essentials of the bank's strategy, within the appropriate limits of confidentiality, need to be continuously communicated throughout the organization by all forms of internal and external media so that in the end it becomes self-fulfilling. In many ways, if all those involved in the bank believe the outcome will be achieved and they have a clearly defined role in that achievement, the psychological motivation is such that it often is.

3.2.9 Time

The final ingredient required for successful planning system introduction is time. Most banks' earliest plans are of poor quality. It is important therefore that sufficient time is given to permit the development of good quality plans which are credible and acceptable to line banking units. Care must be taken during this formative state to nurture, educate, cajole, guide and even coerce line units in their preparation of plans such that this becomes an integral part of their own management activity. Normally it will take at least three plan iterations before a planning system settles down and begins to produce meaningful results.

3.3 WHEN DOES PLANNING FAIL?

Substantial evidence exists on the conditions under which strategic planning systems are seen to fail. You should therefore check to ensure that your system fulfils the following ideals if it is to avoid being seen as unsatisfactory at one or more points in the bank:

— The primary purpose should be to help the author manage his own operations better.

— The second purpose should be to establish a mutually acceptable commitment between the author and his superior.

— The plan must be strategic in orientation.

— It must focus on the critical issues, threats and opportunities which management must address.

— It must identify the action options open and their expected consequences.

— The plan must contain enough of the appropriate information to make it credible.

— It should not be so long as to be unmanageable.

— The plan must be clearly linked with the process of resource allocation.

— Top management must spend adequate time on the process to ensure it is credible to and understood by other managers.

— Planning must be woven into the bank such that it becomes an integral component of the corporate culture.

— Planning should be adjusted to suit the needs of the bank as they evolve over time.

— Rewards and sanctions should not discourage strategic planning by overemphasizing short-term performance measures.

3.4 EVALUATING THE STRATEGIC PLANNING SYSTEM

Check the effectiveness of your strategic planning system by using a planning system audit such as that shown below. In employing such a form remember that different people will interpret the questions in different ways and different evaluations may be given to the same question by people from various parts of the bank. However, such differences can be useful in developing a dialogue on the system and on elements within it which need to be corrected.

The opinions of different people are also not all of equal weight. Thus if the chief executive feels the system fails to produce the appropriate strategic decisions the system clearly needs improvement. However, if the CEO finds it acceptable but other key division managers find it a waste of time or overbureaucratic, this too is a serious cause for concern. The audit should be conducted at various planning levels throughout the bank, with top management evaluating all parts of sections A, B and C but only selected items in sections D and E. These latter sections, however, should be completed by unit and divisional management. When the audit is completed, compare and evaluate the results for the bank as a whole and for the various levels of the management hierarchy. This should lead to discussions and the introduction and testing of methods to improve the shortcomings identified. In this way you will hopefully find that your planning systems will significantly improve your bank's ability to make the appropriate strategic decisions.

Planning system audit[1]

A. *Overall management perceived value*

1. The chief executive officer believes the system helps him to do his job better.

2. Other key line managers find the system useful to them.

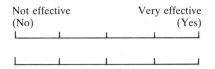

Not effective   Very effective
(No)   (Yes)

[1]Adapted from G. Steiner, *Strategic Planning — What Every Manager Must Know* (New York: Free Press) 1979, pp. 301–303.

3. Overall, the benefits of planning are seen as greater than the costs by most managers.

4. Major changes are needed in the strategic planning systems.

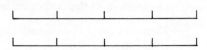

B. *Does the planning system give the 'right' substantive answers and results?*

5. Developing the bank's basic mission and business activities.

6. Foreseeing future major opportunities.

7. Foreseeing future major threats.

8. Properly appraising bank strengths.

9. Properly appraising bank weaknesses.

10. Effectively identifying and evaluating key competitor strategies.

11. Identifying action program priorities.

12. Developing useful long-term objectives.

13. Developing useful long-term strategies.

14. Developing short- and medium-term action programs to implement strategies.

15. Detecting and preventing strategic shocks.

16. Improving the bank's indicators of financial performance:
    Assets
    Liabilities
    Profits
    Return on assets
    Earnings per share

17. The performance of the bank has been better than others not doing comprehensive planning.

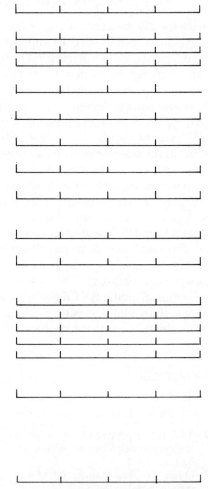

C. *Does the system provide valuable ancillary benefits?*

18. The system has improved the quality of management.

19. The system provides a unifying coordinating force in the bank.

20. The system improves communications and collaboration throughout the bank.

D. *Design of the planning system*

21. Top management has accepted the idea that strategic planning is its major responsibilty.
22. The system fits the management style of the bank.
23. The system fits the needs of the bank's strategic decision-making process.
24. Corporate planning works well with other line managers and staff.
26. The system of reaching strategic decisions works well within the bank.
27. The system uses appropriate understandable concepts for the bank's business.

E. *Are the planning processes effective?*

28. Top management spends an appropriate amount of time on strategic planning.
29. Line managers accept planning and don't just pay lip service to it.
30. Line managers spend an appropriate amount of time in developing strategic plans.
31. The procedures in the plan are acceptable and appropriate.
32. The procedures are well understood within the bank.
33. The workload to complete the plans is acceptable to managers and staff.
34. The process is effective in inducing in-depth strategic thinking.
35. The process is not too routine, inflexible and rigorously numerate.
36. New ideas are generally welcomed.
37. Managers really do face up to bank weaknesses in developing plans.
38. Divisions get sufficient guidance from central office for effective planning.
39. Divisions are encouraged and helped to prepare plans by central office.
40. The ability of managers to undertake planning is taken into account in measuring their performance.

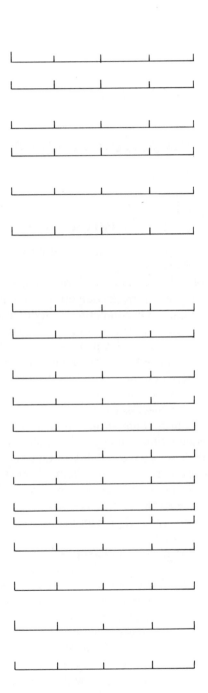

CHAPTER 4

Competitor Analysis

4.1 IMPORTANCE OF COMPETITOR ANALYSIS

The majority of banks operate within a competitive environment. In many markets the degree of competition has been increasing in recent years following the entry of foreign banks. the expansion of domestic ones and the entry of non-bank competitors into traditional banking markets. One result of the growth in competitive activity has been an increasing recognition that the key to business success is more than just the careful analysis of a market and its customers and includes also a detailed analysis of major competitors. Banks have been slow to engage in the former and relatively few have as yet undertaken the latter. Yet in most markets banks that attempt to grow do so most of the time by taking business from an actual or potential competitor and not necessarily through great real growth in the market. Thus, deciding on which competitor to attack or defend against, where, when and how are essential tactical decisions which form a major element in strategic planning. To improve their ability to take the initiative in competitive situations some banks are therefore now following the practice of leading industrial companies and developing competitor intelligence systems. This chapter is designed to assist bank marketing planners and line officers to improve their ability to analyse competitors and so increase their chance of achieving success.

Specifically, understanding and analysing competitors enables you to:

— Plan your strategy so as to neutralize competitor strengths wherever possible, emphasize those services where you are relatively strong, and carefully select accounts where you will have a greater chance of business success.
— Help a potential customer to realistically evaluate your services *versus* those of your competitors.
— Demonstrate with conviction why a customer should choose your bank over that of your competitors.

— Be more confident by increasing your understanding of the relative strengths and weaknesses of your own bank's services.

In seeking corporate banking business you should therefore remember:

— *In gaining new business your initial objective will probably be to become one of a number of banks with which a corporate account does business.* The middle market will be the most heavily contested segment.
— In most cases your gain will be a business loss by one of the existing banks. Only in very rare situations will you actually completely displace an established lead bank relationship and it is often not very profitable to do so if you are a foreign bank.
— You should try to provide those services in which you have a competitive edge and *which are profitable to you* whilst leaving aside those services which are unprofitable to you. This requires you to understand both your own and the competitor's cost structure. Beware of cross-subsidization within your own product range.
— Examine your own accounts carefully and select those to defend because your competitors will be trying to do the same to you as you are doing to their accounts. Remember that at attractive accounts it is usually a buyer's market.

In seeking retail banking business remember:

— Traditionally HNWI accounts have been neglected and used to cross-subsidize poor accounts. In this segment narrow, well-defined attacks from new specialist competitors can be expected.
— Understand your cost structure carefully and identify the costs and benefits associated with each retail segment.
— Select those accounts you wish to service well and match or exceed competitors' service offerings. Be prepared to shed accounts you can't service profitably or which reduce your ability to service your attractive customers.

4.2 DEVELOPING A COMPETITOR INTELLIGENCE SYSTEM

Developing a competitor intelligence system is an important element in strategic and market segment planning. Normally, focused segment attack will not only be based on account or customer cluster plans but also on strategies for dealing with specific competitors. Developing an appropriate intelligence system which examines existing and potential competitors is therefore an important ongoing task conducted at all levels of the bank. The details required and the specific competitors covered will, however, vary according to where in the organization the information is required.

At the corporate level, the competition for analysis will be those banks or other financial institutions it is felt impact most strongly on the bank's overall corporate mission and objectives. For example, competitors studied will normally include all those other local banks drawing funds from the same equity market. Care should be taken, however, not to exclude other competitors outside this area. For example, most US banks compare themselves with other indigenous banks but often fail to examine important international competitors such as those from Britain, Germany, France and Japan. The review of competitor strategies should examine the impact on overall bank mission and objectives and check where the strategic position of particular competitors threatens those. The theme of such analysis therefore tends to be broad in scope, the appropriate time frame being medium to long term.

At the local market level, however, competitors will usually be the indigenous banks in home or host countries within the appropriate geographic served market. At this level details are required of individual bank operational programs, organization, account structure, branch coverage, and the like, with the view to pinpointing appropriate market segment strategies which can be used to penetrate competitor banks' markets.

The corporate and unit systems of competitor intelligence should be integrated and, in addition, should be linked to the account planning process, which is a particular source of information on competitor activities and intentions. The collection of intelligence data is thus a responsibility for everyone in the bank, but specific resources need to be allocated to it, especially at the corporate level, and the results systematically collated. Today such systems are becoming computerized.

4.3 COMPETITOR IDENTIFICATION

In conducting competitor analysis it is necessary to examine those key competitors that presently or in future might be expected to have a significant impact upon your own strategy. Usually this means the inclusion of a wider group of organizations than just your direct competitors. This is likely to be especially true in the banking industry, where major competititve threats will emerge from non-bank financial and industrial corporations. Competitors thus include the following:

Existing direct competitors. Concentrate upon major bank competitors or those with a high growth record, especially when they are operating apparently successful strategies. Note some competitors will not compete with you across the board but in particular products/markets. Different competitors will therefore need to be examined at different levels of depth. Those which already do or could have an ability to substantially impact upon core businesses need closest examination. Be careful not to neglect important competitors which have not been historically significant.

New bank competitors, notably foreign banks or those expanding their domestic geographic coverage.

Potential new market entrants—new non-bank competitors. The major threats facing banks do not necessarily come from direct competitors, who may have much to lose by breaking up established market structures. New competitors include a variety of institutions with an established customer base which can be easily reached by extensions to existing distribution or *via* the use of low-cost technology:

— Firms with low barriers of entry, such as those where entry could make use of shared distribution or systems facilities, a common salesforce, extension to an established brand name and common technology. Examples include major retailers like Sears Roebuck, J. C. Penney and Marks & Spencer or high-technology companies such as IBM and Geisco.

— Firms with a clear experience effect or synergy gain. Examples include American Express/Shearson, Merrill Lynch and Beneficial Finance.

— Forward or backward integrators. Examples include major trading companies such as Inchcape, Mitsui and Mitsubishi. Other examples might include industrial firms such as General Electric and General Motors.

— Unrelated product acquirers where entry offers financial synergy. Examples would include ITT and Bethlehem Steel.

Some firms may enjoy more than one of these advantages.

4.4 SOURCES OF COMPETITOR INTELLIGENCE

Collecting detailed information on competitors is actually surprisingly easy if you approach it systematically and dedicate a relatively limited level of resource to the task. It is surprising, however, how few organizations actually do try to monitor their competitors in other than a financial sense. Key sources of competitive information include the following:

1. *Annual reports and 10ks,* and where available the annual reports or returns of subsidiaries/business units.

2. *Competitive product literature.*

3. *Bank internal newspapers and magazines.* These can be very useful for details of all major appointments, staff background profiles, business unit descriptions, statements of philosophy, new branches and services and activities, and strategic moves.

4. *Bank and company histories.* These volumes are very useful to gain an understanding of the organizational culture, the rationale for the existing position and details of the internal systems and politics.

5. *Advertising.* This illustrates and identifies themes, choice of media, spend level and the timing of specific strategies.

6. *Bank directories.* These are an excellent source for identifying organization, mode of customer service, depth of specialist segment coverage, attitudes to specific activities and relative power positions.

7. *Financial industry press.* Most banks make use of the financial press for announcements and this is a very useful source for details of all significant changes in products, prices, sales and marketing persoinnel, new units and investments. Also, check bank press releases if available. Libraries such as the *Financial Times'* will have most of these and will allow access to library service subscribers.

8. *Financial, national and international press.* These sources are useful for bank financial and strategic announcements and analysis and senior personnel/organization announcements. Specialist agencies such as McCarthy may provide a clippings service to obviate the need for internal press monitoring. A check of the local press where the competitor has major branches, subsidiaries, divisional or corporate headquarters is also useful when the competitor's activity is significant relative to the area. This is especially true in the US, where local coverage is often all there is on regional banks. Funk and Scott provide an international index. Index facilities are available for *WSJ, NY Times, The Times, Financial Times, Frankfurter Allemande, Euromoney, The Banker,* etc.

9. *Papers and speeches of corporate executives.* These are useful for details of internal procedures, organization, senior management philosophy and strategic intentions.

10. *Account officer/branch manager.* Although often biased, used and directed systematically, intelligence reports from field officers provide front-line market intelligence on competitors, customers, prices, products, service, quality, delivery, and the like.

11. *Customers.* Reports from customers can be actively solicited internally or obtained *via* external market research agencies and provide first-hand market intelligence. The corporate banking industry places heavy reliance on Greenwich Research Associates, where the methodology is on occasion suspect. Few banks do enough systematic market research but good

success has been reported with individual customer studies, focus groups, and the like.

12. *Suppliers.* Reports from suppliers are especially useful in assessing investment plans, activity levels, efficiency, etc. This is particularly true of systems products, which are likely to be of increased importance.

13. *Professional advisers.* Many banks are making active use of consultants to improve their strategic planning, cost control and marketing systems. Who these consultants are will usually tell you a great deal about the sort of systems and procedures the bank is likely to adopt.

14. *Stockbrokers' reports.* These often provide useful operational details usually obtained from internal information coupled with financial analysis. Similarly, industry studies may provide useful information about specific competitors within a particular country or region. For US banks, Keefe, Bruyette and Woods specialize in a great variety of bank financial and other data.

15. *Bank association and society contacts.* The industry is one where formal associations such as the ABA and Institute of Bankers are primary forums for discussion. Education programs, informal discussions and the like are major opportunities to learn about competitors' activities and procedures. The present frankness which pervades these may reduce as bank industry competition intensifies and approaches that found in other industries.

16. *Competitor service analysis.* Look closely at the services offered by competitors but be careful not to just search for *negative* characteristics in them. Try to be objective, possibly using external panels, and look carefully at service features *superior* to your own which can be copied, modified or improved upon.

17. *Recruited competitor personnel.* There is substantial movement of personnel within the industry and such moves can be systematically used to improve information on competitor activities and operations. Remember, in developing and introducing a new service rather than inventing it from scratch internally it is often cheapest to hire a key person from a successful service-innovating bank or company.

18. *Retired executive consultants.* Retired executives from competitors can often be hired as consultants, and information about their former employers can be effectively determined by requesting their assistance in specific job areas.

4.5 COMPETITOR ANALYSIS DATA BASE

In order to evaluate competitor strengths and weaknesses, it is necessary to systematically collect data on each significant actual or potential competitor. The most important competitors should be comprehensively and continuously monitored. For those organizations which are a less direct immediate threat annual periodic reviews are acceptable, but be ready to upgrade your analysis when appropriate. The data to collect should include:

1. Name of competitor bank or potential competitor.
2. Number and location of offices, branches, operations complexes, non-bank subsidiaries.
3. Number and nature of personnel attached to each unit.
4. Details of bank organization and business unit structure.
5. Financial details of bank group and individual bank and non-bank business units, stock market assessment, details of major shareholders, potential acquirers/acquisitions.
6. Corporate and business unit growth rate, profitability.
7. Details of service range, including pricing, and service quality.
8. Details of market share by segment, by geography.
9. Details of advertising and promotion, spending levels, timing, media choice, promotions, advertising support.
10. Details of line and branch field operations, including numbers, organization responsibilities, special procedures for key accounts, any team selling capabilities such as multinational corporations, means of integrating related banking services, operations based services such as personal banking, small corporate, middle market, multinationals.
11. Details of major customer segments served, key accounts. Estimates of customer loyalty, relative market image.
12. Details of specialist markets served such as real estate, energy, shipping, project finance, Euromarket syndication.
13. Details of research and development spending, facilities, development themes, special skills and attributes, geographic coverage.
14. Details of operations and systems facilities, capacity size, scale, age, utilization, assessment of output efficiency, capital intensity, replacement policies.
15. Details of key suppliers.
16. Details of personnel numbers, personnel relations record, relative efficiency and productivity, salary rates, rewards and sanctions policies, degree of unionization.
17. Details of key individuals within the bank/individual business units.
18. Details of control, information and planning systems.

4.6 ANALYSING COMPETITOR STRATEGY

The strategy of key competitors should be analysed and evaluated with a view to assessing their *relative* strengths and weaknesses in order to identify strategic alternatives for your bank and establish likely competitor responses to your own strategic moves. Most large banks today are multibusiness concerns so competitor strategy needs to be evaluated at several levels, including:

1. *By function.*

2. *By business unit.* A business unit is normally a fully developed business activity which contains within it all the necessary functions to be measured and monitored as a separate profit center. However, definitions of a business unit differ widely, and it is quite possible that some competitor banks may not include all the same aspects of a specific business in their definition as you do. Indeed, in many banks the concept of business units is still new and relatively undeveloped and as a consequence many have inadequate knowledge of costs structures, customer segmentation, and the like.

3. *By the bank corporation as a whole.* The modern large bank corporation is usually made up of a portfolio of businesses each of which may be required to perform a different task in meeting the corporate objectives and strategy. At present most banks do not operate a portfolio system because their internal planning is not adequately developed. While this may yield a significant competitive advantage to well-disciplined banks, it can lead to apparently irrational competitive behavior.

4.6.1 Function Analysis

For each particular business, identify and evaluate the main functional strategies of key competitors using a format such as the following. It will often not be possible to be strictly accurate but careful study and constant revue of key competitors will usually allow you to guestimate relative differences whenever these are significant. While identifying specific functional policies of each competitor also track trends in these policies over time and look carefully for any significant changes and the reasons for them.

Marketing Strategy

1. What service strategy is adopted by each competitor relative to yours? What is the market size by product market/customer segment? What is the market share by competitor by segment?

2. What is the growth rate by service market/customer segment? What is the growth rate of each competitor by service line/customer segment?

3. What is the service line strategy of each competitor?

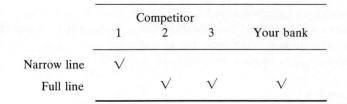

	Competitor			
	1	2	3	Your bank
Narrow line	√			
Full line		√	√	√

4. What is the policy toward new services adopted by each competitor? What has been the rate of new service introduction in the past five years? What particular approaches to new service launches have been used consistently?

		Competitor			
		1	2	3	Your bank
Service line	A	L	F	—	F
	B	L	F	F	F
	C	F	F	F	L

L, leader; F, follower.

5. What is the relative service quality of each competitor by service line compared to yours?

		Competitor			
		1	2	3	Yours
Service line	A	S	I	—	S
	B	S	A	I	A
	C	S	A	I	A

S, superior; A, average; I, inferior.

6. What pricing strategy does each competitor adopt by service line/consumer?

		Competitor			
		1	2	3	Yours
Service line	A	H	L	—	A
	B	A	A	A	A
	C	H	A	L	H

H, higher than average; A, average price; L, lower than average.

7. What are the relative advertising and promotion strategies of each competitor?

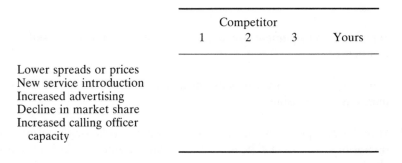

Total expenditure	Competitor			
	1	2	3	Yours
As percentage of deposits				
By geographic region				
By customer segment				
By media type				
By month				
By season				

8. For wholesale businesses, what are the customer servicing strategies of each competitor and how do these compare?

9. What do you believe the marketing objectives of each competitor to be?

10. How quickly is each competitor able to modify its marketing policies to meet a new entry situation? In what way has such modification occurred in the past?

	Competitor			
	1	2	3	Yours
Lower spreads or prices				
New service introduction				
Increased advertising				
Decline in market share				
Increased calling officer capacity				

11. How do operations/credit/marketing/selling fit into each competitor's organization? Has marketing historically been a background for any key executives/chief executives? How does this compare with credit?

Operations Strategy

1. What are the number, size and location of each competitor's branches and offices? How do these compare with one another? What service range does each offer? What is the estimated capacity of each service range by competitor, e.g. estimated total loan capacity for given equity base, estimated transaction capacity for given computer capability?

2. What is each competitor's actual volume? Capacity utilization?

3. What is the level of each competitor's capital employed in depreciable capital equipment? Owned property? How does each of these compare to equity capital?

4. How many people are employed by branch/office? By businesses? By subsidiary? What wages are paid?

5. What is the relative loans and services output/capital employed for each competitor?

6. What is the loans and services output per employee for each competitor? What is the relative employee cost?

7. What is the degree of unionization for each competitor? What is the relative record for labor unrest for each competitor?

8. What percentage of liabilities is supplied from other internal business sources? What percentage of output is supplied to internal businesses?

9. What service costs do you estimate each competitor has relative to your own?

10. What man-management/organization incentive systems are used by each competitor?

11. What services if any are subcontracted for each competitor? Is this increasing/decreasing?

12. How does operations fit into each competitor's organization? Has operations historically been a major background for key executives/ chief executives?

13. How flexible is each competitor to a change in market conditions service volume? What have been typical historic responses to fluctuating demand?

Dimensions of Product/Service Development

1. Where are new services developed?

2. What is the estimated new service development expenditure level of each competitor relative to yours? How has this changed over the past three years?

3. How many people are employed at each competitor in specialist service development? How many of these do you estimate are qualified?

4. What is the record of each competitor in service introduction/product improvement over the past five years?

5. How rapidly can each competitor respond to another's new service introductions? What sort of reaction has traditionally been evoked?

Financial Strategy

1. What is the financial performance of each competitor for this business in terms of return on assets/cash flow/spread/loan loss rate?

2. What is the dividend/payout ratio of this business for each competitor? Are funds being extracted in any other way? Is cash being injected in any other way than from operations?

3. What is the calculated sustainable growth rate based on existing equity base?

4. What are the liabilities needs of this business in its present position? What flexibility does the business have for improving its funds utilization? What are the most sensitive variables for using/relaxing cash?

5. What liabilities/other funds sources are open for this business?

6. How does each competitor's growth rate compare with average industry rate (with and without allowance for inflation)? In the event of a shortage of adequate deposit base what additional capital resources are available? What would be the cost of these funds? What alternative uses might have priority for these funds?

7. How adaptable is each competitor's liabilities management to changing market conditions such as rising interest rates, increased inflation, rising wage costs? What typical reactions has each competitor made historically to such events?

4.6.2 Business Unit Objectives

The starting point for evaluating each competitor bank at the market segment/business unit level is to assess what is expected of the strategic business unit (SBU). This will not be spelt out for you but will be apparent from a variety of factors such as management speeches, choice of managers to run the unit, top management attitudes to the unit, amount of resources allocated, and the like. In assessing the objectives of a business unit the following questions are helpful.

1. What are the stated (and unstated but obvious from management actions) financial objectives for the business in terms of return on assets, cash flow and market share penetration?
2. What is management's attitude to risk? How are profits/market share/asset growth and unit risk balanced?
3. What non-economic objectives, values or beliefs prevail? How, where and when do these supersede economic objectives? Typical non-economic values/objectives might be as follows:

    'People's bank': Sanwa Bank
    'Pacific Rim market leader': Security Pacific
    'World's largest merchant bank': J. P. Morgan
    'Trendsetting innovator': Citibank

4. What is the competitor business unit organization structure? How are key decision responsibilities allocated? How well are separate functions coordinated within the business unit? Between this business unit and others which are integrated with it? Organizational differences are a key distinguishing feature between banks and lack of inter and intra business unit coordination is a principal reason for competitive weakness.
5. What control and incentive systems operate? What behavior is rewarded/sanctioned? What is the nature of the existing incentive/sanction system? Again significant differences between banks may be identified. Relatively few have well-developed cost systems for example and few presently offer significant variable reward schemes which are related to quantified performance goals.
6. What kinds of managers lead the competitor SBU? What are their backgrounds and experience? What is the make-up/style/skills/background of junior managers?
7. What social/government/union/legal constraints on behavior occur in this business?
8. Where does the SBU fit into the bank group organization structure? Who does the SBU head report to? Check.
    — Direct to CEO/chairman
    — To senior executive VP
    — To divisional executive with influence
    — To corporate hitman
    — Other (specify)
9. What is the status of the SBU head? Check.
    — Sharetaker
    — Caretaker
    — Undertaker

10. What economic relationships exist between this SBU and others in the bank portfolio? Check:
    — Source of funds
    — Use of funds
    — Integrated operations
    — Geographic integration
    — Horizontal integration
11. Do integrated relationships affect strategic behavior within the SBU? Check for:
    — Cross-subsidization
    — Profit movement/transfer to other SBUs
    — Unit hold/grow strategy to protect/help other SBUs
12. Does this SBU enjoy sacred cow status? Likely signs are positive answers to any of the following:
    — Are any former SBU heads in top management positions?
    — Was this SBU one of the bank's earliest businesses?
    — Does the SBU have special emotional appeal to top management?
    — Was the SBU originally developed by the present top management?
13. How does the performance of this SBU compare with that of the bank as a whole?
    — Underperformers are usually under pressure
    — Overperformers are usually pampered
14. Why did the parent enter this business? Check:
    — To exploit global network
    — Pressure from customers/competitors
    — Planned diversification move
    — Random chance or accident
    — Personal whim of senior management
15. What is the strategic importance of this business to the parent bank? Is it a core business or peripheral to the bank's major activity? Where does the SBU appear to fit in a corporate portfolio? Check the portfolio strategy position:
    — Growth
    — Maintenance
    — Harvest
    — Divest
16. Where does the SBU fit in bank diversification strategy? Is the bank diversifying and directing financial people/resources in this direction or away from it? Will its diversification moves help/hinder this SBU?

4.6.3 Bank Group Business Objectives

Companies also need to be evaluated at the level of the total bank corporation or group. Surprisingly, perhaps, a variety of factors which influence the entire bank

group will significantly influence behavior at the SBU level. An understanding
of group attitudes and strategy is therefore a requisite component in evaluating
competitor strategies and designing countermeasures. This is especially true
for key competitors faced in a global arena. At the group level try to evaluate
the following factors:

1. What are the the overall group financial objectives? Check the impact of:
   — Inflation
   — Technology change
   — Wage costs
   — Foreign exchange rates
   — Interest rates
   — Capital needs
   — Equity costs
2. What is the competitor's growth capability? Check.
   — What is short-run growth capacity?
   — What is long-run growth capacity?
   — What is financially sustainable growth rate?
   — How does competitor's strategic capability change with growth?
3. What are the competitor's key strengths and weaknesses?
   — What capability changes seem likely?
4. How adaptable is the competitor's overall strategy? Check:
   — What is fixed *vs* variable cost structure? Cost of unused capacity?
     Influence on strategic change capability?
   — What is competitor's ability to adapt to functional change?
     • Ability to compete on cost
     • Ability to introduce new services
     • Ability to increase marketing support
   — What is competitor's ability to adapt to environmental change?
     Check adaptability to:
     • Sustained high inflation
     • Technological change
     • Recession
     • Higher wage costs
     • Changing regulatory environment domestically/interna-
       tionally
5. Can you sketch the competitor's business portfolio?
   — Don't forget to use *his* classification scheme
   — Identify relative SBU positions and size from the competitor's
     perspective
   — Use a similar three by three matrix to that in Chapter 2 (Figure
     4.1). Score competitor business units in the same way as you did
     your own.
The matrix summary can also be utilized to show the expected trends in

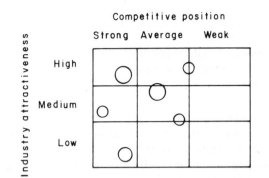

Figure 4.1   Competitor portfolio matrix

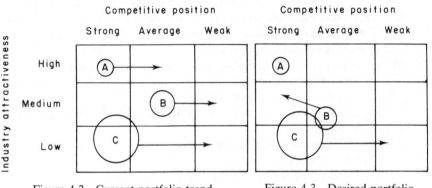

Figure 4.2   Current portfolio trend

Figure 4.3   Desired portfolio objective

position if no changes are made in strategy (Figure 4.2) and the apparent desired competitor trend (Figure 4.3).

6. Interrogate the competitor's business portfolio by asking:
   — Which businesses stabilize the portfolio?
   — Which are the core businesses?
   — Which are the growth businesses?
   — Which are the problem businesses?
   — Check if competitor appears to be following the suggested investment strategy for specific business. Check if not then why not?
   — Which businesses defend the core businesses?
   — Which businesses look most promising for further investment?
   — Which have the greatest 'leverage' on bank performance?
   — Which businesses are employed as attack businesses or could be used to reduce another competitor's strength?
7. What does the competitor bank appear to believe about his relative market position? Check relative position on:

— Costs, notably funds, premises, people, systems
— Service quality
— Technology/skills capability
— Marketing/selling capability
— Price
— Account penetration
— Account solicitation

Assess these positions from public statements, service/media claims, and the like. Are these views realistic?

8. Does the competitor appear to follow any generic strategies? E.g. Barclays Group—multiple office, consumer orientation, international credit finance.

9. Are there any strongly inculcated cultural norms which affect corporate behavior? Note especially any norms established by the company founder. E.g. Deutsche Bank—resistance to consumer credit cards; Citicorp—reluctance to take direct equity stakes.

10. What are the prevailing values/aspirations of top management? E.g.:
    — Does the bank seek to be a technical leader or follower, e.g. Citicorp *vs* Bank of America?
    — Does the bank seek to deal with only a limited customer base, e.g. J. P. Morgan?

11. Are there cultural/regional/national differences which affect ways each competitor perceives and acts? E.g.
    — German banks are universal investment/commercial banking institutions
    — Japanese banks are closely related to formal or informal corporate customer groups
    — American banks outside California are corporate *vs* retail in orientation
    — British banks are branch and retail oriented

12. Does the competitor have strong historical or emotional ties to particular businesses/services/policies? How strongly will these ties be maintained? Are they valid assumptions?

13. What is the current performance of the competitor compared with the past? Banks will try to regain past glories if they exist.

14. Where has the competitor failed previously? Banks will try to avoid areas of past failure.

15. Where has the competitor previously been successful? Banks will often try to repeat past successes.

16. How has the competitor reacted to earlier competitive moves? Emotionally? Rationally? Slowly? Quickly?

17. What is the experience background of top management, e.g. domestic branch banking, international corporate banking, credit finance, etc.? Internal *vs* external appointments? This background will probably influence their strategic direction and interests.

18. What strategies have previously worked for top management? What strategies have previously failed for them? Successful strategies will often be tried again and failing strategies avoided.
19. What other businesses have top management worked in? How successful were they? Why did they leave? This history will also influence their strategic behavior, e.g. Aboud at First Chicago.
20. What major events have top management lived through which might influence them, e.g. German bank management attitudes to inflation?
21. What attitudes do top management portray in their speeches/writings? What are their interests/pastimes and how do these influence their behavior, e.g. Rockefeller at Chase?
22. Who advises top management? What strategic patterns have these advisors installed in other companies, e.g. McKinsey at Continental Illinois, Boston Consulting Group at Bank of America, General Electric at Chase Manhattan?
23. What sort of executives seem to get on in the competitor?
24. How fast do managers move in and out of SBUs? How is performance rewarded/sanctioned?
25. What does the competitor appear to believe about future demand and industry trends? How well has the competitor estimated in the past?
26. What does the competitor appear to believe about its competitors? Are there any over or under estimations?

4.7 ASSESSING COMPETITOR STRATEGIC CAPABILITY

The objective of conducting competitor analysis is to identify likely competitor strategies and responses to strategic moves adopted by you. In most industries success is dependent on gaining an edge on competitors and this type of evaluation is therefore as important as basic market or customer analysis. Assessing competitor strategic capability involves taking the answers to the above checklists and attempting the following:

1. From the analysis of competitive goals, present strategy and capabilities, assess:
   — What are the likely competitor offensive moves? Use the *competitor's* assumed logic, not your own.
   — What are the competitor's likely defensive strategic capabilities?
   — What would be the best battleground on which to tackle the competitor?
2. Evaluate competitor offensive strategies:
   — Given the competitor's present strategic position and goals, how likely is he to start an offensive strategy?
   — Which offensive moves seem most likely?
   — What gains can the competitor expect to make from these moves? Short term? Long term?

3. Evaluate competitor defensive strategies:
   — What moves is the competitor most vulnerable to?
   — What moves will provoke maximum/minimum retaliatory action from the competitor? Which will result in the most unprofitable retaliation? For him? For you?
   — What moves is each competitor least able to respond to quickly/effectively?
   — What 'blind spots' does the competitor have which would provoke low retaliation probability?
4. Assess your goals and strategy:?
   — What positions allow you to meet your objectives without excess threat/retaliation from competitors; e.g. it is relatively easy to gain market share against a competitor harvesting a business providing this does not prevent the competitor achieving his ROA objectives.

4.8 SUMMARY

The competitor intelligence system of the bank is an important ingredient in the development of market and corporate strategy. The relative competitive position of the bank needs to be systematically established as a component in the allocation of market investment strategy. Check the analysis of the appropriate competitors at corporate, division or market level using the following checklist:
1. Are the appropriate competitors correctly identified?
2. Are all major competitive new entries identified, including non-banks?
3. Have all appropriate sources of competitor intelligence been reviewed?
4. Is the data base on each competitor adequate for competitor analysis? Are any essential data missing and, if so, where can they be obtained, how, by when and at what cost?
5. Has the analysis of each key bank function been undertaken at the appropriate level for each market segment?
6. Is the competitor business unit strategy adequately identified? Is its position within the competitor bank's overall portfolio assessed realistically?
7. Have the business units' objectives been determined adequately?
8. Are the competitor bank's overall mission and objectives identified?
9. Has the competitor's market portfolio been developed and interrogated adequately?
10. Have the competitor's culture, organization, leadership and history been analysed and the impact of these factors on strategy been assessed?
11. Has the competitor's strategic capability been assessed and likely offensive and defensive strategic moves identified?
12. Have your bank's relative strengths and weaknesses been assessed realistically and the most appropriate strategic moves to adopt against specific competitors identified?

CHAPTER 5

Purchasing Financial Services

5.1 BASIC PURCHASE MOTIVATION

Purchasing behavior is triggered into action by the recognition of 'needs' or 'wants' which stimulate an urge or drive to take action which will lead to the 'satisfaction' of the need. This process is referred to as 'motivation'. The process applies to the individual and in a more complex form in organizations. Understanding how people are motivated therefore helps you to:

— identify future customer needs more effectively;
— improve your bank's ability to communicate with potential customers in terms they can understand;
— emphasize those features of your bank's service that will be likely to have the most appeal;
— plan marketing strategy to produce the desired results;
— obtain the confidence of customers by showing how your bank understands their point of view.

What you need to know is: Who buys? How do they buy? When do they buy? Where do they buy? and Why do they buy? Changing technology and the development of alternative delivery systems are providing a growing choice of possibilities to both individual and corporate customers, making an understanding of customer behavior even more important. As illustrated in Figure 5.1, buyers respond to external stimuli with specific patterns of behavior. The role of marketing is to understand the intervening process which influences buying decisions.

5.1.1 The Purchase Decision Process

Customer behavior is influenced by a number of cultural, social, personal and pyschological factors. For individual bank customers the emotional and pyschological factors tend to be more important, while industrial and corporate purchasing tends to be substantially more rational. It would be incorrect,

External stimuli		Buying process		Buying behavior	
Marketing	*Environment*			Service	Choice
Product	Social	Buyer	Buying	Bank	Choice
Price	Political	needs	decision	Service	Timing
Place	Technological $\rightarrow$	objectives	process $\rightarrow$	Service	Amount
Promotion	Economic			Service	Frequency
	Cultural				

Figure 5.1 The buying decision process

however, to assume that emotional factors do not influence corporate buying behavior.

External factors influencing buying behavior include the following:

1. *Culture*. The society in which both the individual and corporations develop significantly influences behavior. Attitudes to risk, degree of competitiveness, efficiency, degree of individualism, personal freedom, pursuit of success and the like are all key values significantly influenced by the culture in which we exist. Moreover, most of us also belong to subcultures within the wider society. For example, ethnic groups, regional differences, climatic and religious differences can all influence behavior. Similarly, each corporate organization tends to have its own internal subculture influenced by its own history, the participants, established norms and practices and company's leadership.
2. *Reference groups*. Individuals and corporations are also usually members of various groups which in turn influence behavior. Primary groups with which an individual interacts regularly include family, neighbors and fellow workers. Secondary groups can include professional association memberships, trade unions, trade associations and industry confederations. It is an important element in marketing strategy for banks to identify and reach those opinion leaders in appropriate reference groups for personal and corporate clients to gain service endorsements which can be used in the relevant personal or media communication channels.
3. *Personal factors*. Personal factors influence the type of service required, the location of purchase, the price to be paid and how to reach the individual. While personal factors are critical for retail banking, they also influence the corporate decision purchasing process. Significant personal factors include:
   (a) age and life-cycle stage;
   (b) occupation;
   (c) economic status, including disposable income, savings and assets, borrowing power and attitude to spending *vs* saving;
   (d) lifestyle.

4. *Organizational factors.* Each corporation has its own structure, systems, procedures, objectives, politics and individual personalities. These factors will all blend together to influence the corporate buying decision process.

The reasons for utilizing specific bank services reflect the desire to satisfy both rational and emotional needs on the part of both the individual and the corporation. The principal emotional motivators which apply in both individual and corporate purchase situations include the following:

1. *Ego enhancement.* Individuals have a need for achievement and personal recognition. People want to be appreciated, to be complimented, to be made to feel important.
2. *Personal power and influence.* Individuals have a need for personal power and influence; to be able to dominate and control their immediate environment and to achieve increased success.
3. *Personal risk reduction.* Organizational purchasers are by nature somewhat risk-averse and need to feel reassured that any services contemplated do not place them at an unacceptable level of personal risk.
4. *Personal gain or profit.* This can be an emotional as well as a rational motivation. The motive of pecuniary gain has two phases — the one prompts the buyer to spend money to make money, a positive implication, while the other is concerned with the *saving* of money, a negative implication.
5. *Desire for affiliation.* In addition to a desire to be recognized, individuals to a greater or lesser degree want to be liked and socially accepted by others.
6. *Physical and aesthetic pleasure.* The satisfaction of basic physical needs is the most fundamental human drive, while the satisfaction of aesthetic needs is one of a higher order but which can also be an important influence upon the individual.

Similarly, the key rational purchase motivations include:

1. *Profit or economy.* Profit is probably the dominant motive in most commercial enterprises. For non-profit organizations, while the concept of profit may not be relevant, economies will still be important motivators in the form of cost reductions or savings on existing operations. For individuals, costs and interest rate margins are also extremely important although the inertia effect tends to be much stronger.
2. *Flexibility.* Services which are flexible or can be adjusted and adapted to meet changing needs appeal to the motive of flexibility.
3. *Speed.* Services which increase speed of operation may be especially attractive to some corporations by reducing funding needs, improving cash flow and accelerating payments. The speed with which services can be introduced and benefits provided can also be an important motivator. Speed credits tend to be popular with consumers, but direct debits are not necessarily attractive unless accompanied by financial advantages like lower prices.

4. *Service quality*. Price or cost is by no means always the key determining factor in the choice of services purchased either by individuals or corporations. Perceived quality of service is one of the most important factors governing choice, and indeed in many cases too low a price might well have a negative effect on perceived service expectations.
5. *Protection and security*. Company personnel are influenced by service features which will protect the company's property or its employees. Individuals too need security and rely heavily on banks to be safe repositories for deposits.
6. *Back-up service*. Most companies are not merely concerned with the short term when purchasing banking services, but rather with a long-term relationship. As a result, back-up service is important to ensure that benefits obtained are continuous and not merely temporary.
7. *Convenience*. Geographic and/or organizational convenience may be secondary motivators in the choice of bank. This is especially true for mobile individuals.
8. *Reputation and perceived technical skill*. The reputation and perceived technical skill of a bank are important motivators in assessing whether its services are considered credible by both individuals and corporate accounts. Most corporate decision-makers are by nature conservative and will not tend to take risks with institutions of unknown reputation in areas of activity such as banking services. Consumers tend to be even more risk-averse, although a fringe segment can usually be lured into making investments in dubious institutions. It is such investors that the regulatory authorities are always at pains to protect.

5.2 SPECIFIC NEEDS AND WANTS

The basic motives outlined above describe the factors that will help convince prospective customers that they should do business with your bank. To be of value in marketing planning these basic motives must be analysed and defined in terms of specific needs and wants that the bank is capable of satisfying.

The key task therefore is to develop a checklist of the specific needs and wants which you believe influence the decision-making process in each major account and then plan to satisfy these needs.

For example, the criteria used for the selection of lead banks by large multinational corporations (MNCs) have been identified as shown in Table 5.1.

MNCs from the US and Western Europe tend to have somewhat different emphases in their choice of lead banks. American MNCs attach great importance to global branch network cover, to the bank being their lead domestic bank and to it having account executives knowledgeable in international services. By contrast, European MNCs emphasize foreign exchange services and relative efficiency in international operating services as

Table 5.1
Criteria Used in Selecting Lead Banks by MNCs (%)

Criterion	US MNCs	European MNCs
Have global branch network	57	44
Have officers knowledgeable in international services	34	N/A
Have as domestic lead bank	32	24
Are efficient in international operating services	28	46
Have high-quality forex services	27	49
Provide most foreign credit needs	26	21
Have outstanding specialists in wide range of international services	24	N/A
Have ability to meet multicurrency borrowing needs	21	N/A
Are competitive in pricing international credit services	19	38
Are efficient in international money transfer services	19	26
Have strong reputation among foreign governments and banks	13	N/A
Have strong international cash management services	9	12

Source: Greenwich Research Associates.

well as a global branch network. Moreover, European MNCs seem much more concerned with competitive pricing than their US counterparts. The relative difference in emphasis reflects in part the strategic differences between MNCs from the two continents. US MNCs tend to be more concerned with the operation of a global strategy, with substantial product interflows across national boundaries. European MNCs, however, are presently much less organized on an integrated global basis and many of their subsidiaries tend to operate purely within local rather than regional or global markets.

While these criteria apply to MNC parent companies, their subsidiary companies operating in Europe or North America use somewhat different ones for the selection of lead banks for operations within their host countries. The criteria used by subsidiary companies are shown in Table 5.2.

The subsidiaries of European MNCs emphasize four criteria in selecting lead banks:

— The provision of most credit needs
— Quality operating services
— Flexibility in tailoring services
— Efficient international money transfer services

Table 5.2:
Criteria used in Selecting lead Banks by Subsidiary Companies (%)

Criterion	European subsidiaries in US	American subsidiaries In Europe
Provide most credit needs	42	31
Have high-quality operating services	36	44
Are flexible in tailoring services	34	42
Are efficient in international operating money transfer services	32	30
Are parent company's worldwide lead bank	27	21
Have high-quality forex services	27	41
Have most attractive loan pricing	22	28
Have knowledge of US financial conditions	19	23
Have global branch network	15	26
Have officers knowledgeable in international services	13	30
Have good reputation among local firms	12	7
Are innovative and imaginative in providing credit	11	11
Are efficient in international cash management	7	10

Source: Greenwich Research Associates.

American MNC subsidiaries are even more concerned with operating service quality, flexibility in tailoring services, foreign exchange services and international services knowledge.

The differing levels of importance of various services illustrated above demonstrate the need to examine carefully the precise characteristics of individual target accounts and to plan in detail the marketing approach to be adopted.

5.3 CORPORATE PURCHASING PROCESS

The decision to 'purchase' corporate banking services involves interactions between at least two individuals, one from the bank and the other from the customer organization. The most usual contact between the bank and the customer is the finance director or corporate treasurer, but in large accounts it may be difficult to gain the attention of the top finance executive in the customer organization.

While the personal motivation of the financial officer is extremely important, it is also essential for the banker to recognize that his personal interaction with the treasurer is not the only interaction which takes place. The treasurer is subject to a variety of influences within his own organization and significant decisions regarding banking arrangements are usually the subject of discussion at board or board committee level. It is therefore necessary to bear the following points in mind:

— The decision to purchase financial services will often be taken by a number of influencers who may not actually understand the technical nature of the services.

— The corporate financial officer will act as a surrogate 'salesman' for the banker. While there is a tendency for non-financial executives to be strongly influenced by the financial specialist this is not always the case, and bankers should also strive to gain the support of other key influencers.

— Financial officers are *not* professional purchasing agents. Emotional motivations may therefore tend to be somewhat more important than with professional purchasing agents.

— Financial services are seen as support facilities and *not* as primary supplies for a company. Banking service decisions are thus often *tertiary* factors, made *after* primary decisions on which businesses to invest in, etc.

— To contribute significantly in meeting the needs of executives engaged in operations who can influence the choice of banking services, the banker should aim to become involved in operating decision-making at an early stage.

— Bankers must think in terms of 'buying centers' rather than individual customers for financial services. The individuals involved in the buying center should be identified, their role understood and the criteria they use in decision-making established.

— The decision-making on financial services varies within industrial groups in line with the organization of the corporate treasury function. It may well be a multitier decision process where, for example, the banking services used by an MNC subsidiary may result from a decision involving treasury executives in several parts of the organization in several countries. The 'sale' of banking services may therefore involve a joint or team marketing approach and require coordination within the bank that cuts across established organizational boundaries.

— An important criterion for many large accounts in selecting bankers is that the calling officer should appear to have the power to negotiate or at least be able to 'sell' any deal within the bank. Without this power he may well lack credibility.

5.4 THE ORGANIZATION OF THE CORPORATE TREASURY FUNCTION

An understanding of the way in which corporations organize the corporate treasury function is useful, and depending upon how this is conducted so the approach to individual accounts may vary.

The organization of the corporate treasury function varies in relation to a number of factors, including:

— Size
— Degree of geographic diversification
— Degree of product diversification
— Role of product diversification
— Number and location of sites/subsidiaries
— Formal corporate structure

In particular, international activities have an important effect on the corporate treasury function. In addition to the range of problems faced in one-country trading, the parent headquarters' treasurer in an MNC must cope with problems such as international taxation rates, remittance policies, foreign exchange exposure, local capital market variations, exchange control restrictions and different legal and accounting conventions. He must probably also coordinate separate finance/treasury functions in a number of other countries which by their nature will enjoy some degree of local autonomy in the choice of banks and banking services.

Three particular modes of treasury management have been identified. The elementary organization which is found in companies with limited international activity is also similar to a relatively diversified domestic organization. The three forms are illustrated below, together with the conditions under which each structure is most commonly found.

1. Elementary international treasury organization

This is illustrated in Figure 5.2. It is usually found where there is:

— Low level of international activity
— Little or no international trading across geographic borders
— Domestic organizational structure functional or possibly divisional, or an overseas holding company structure

This system allows substantial autonomy amongst the subsidiaries of the corporation and there is little or no central coordination of the financial and cash systems. The appointment of banks may be ultimately subject to approval at the central office of the parent company, but it is worth contacting subsidiaries since the financial officers in these will have significant opportunities to influence decision and for many services may be able to appoint banks on their own initiative.

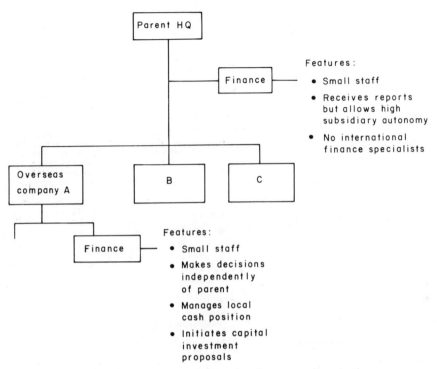

Figure 5.2   Elementary international treasury organization

2. Intermediate international treasury organization

This is illustrated in Figure 5.3. It is usually found where there is:

— Modest levels of international activity (*c.* 15–40 per cent of sales) with some intercompany activity
— With all forms of international organization structure, but common with international division type organizations
— Previous history of serious international loss in a subsidiary, especially due to foreign exchange losses or uncovered devaluation
— Corporate financial staff who have responsibility for both domestic and international operations. Global financial planning is *not* conducted

To gain acceptance as a banker to companies organized in this way, it is often essential to be appointed *via* the parent company central finance function, except for basic local banking services. Subsidiary companies have little or no autonomy and the only services which may be used tend to be transaction/operating type or other services coordinated under guidelines laid down by the corporate center. The key target for account planning is therefore the central treasury and until a favorable position is developed here it is seldom

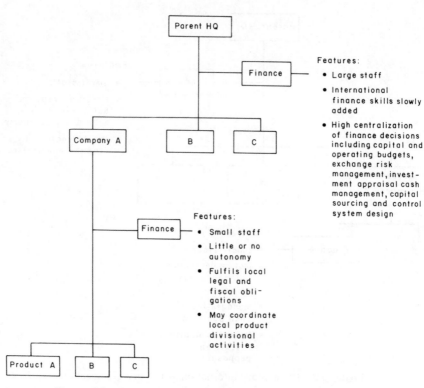

Figure 5.3   Intermediate international treasury organization

worthwhile to spend expensive account officer time trying to penetrate at subsidiary units.

3. Advanced international treasury organization

This is illustrated in Figure 5.4. It is usually found where there is:

— High level of geographic and product diversity. High intercompany trading activity between overseas subsidiaries as well as with the parent
— Controlled decentralization within a well-developed set of corporate rules
— With matrix area-based organization structures. Finance function becomes three-tier
— Large, international financial skills, including specialist tax advice, treasury and controllership

This type of organization has multiple banking relationships usually with many local and international banks. The ultimate appointment of banks is often authorized by the central treasury but recommendations are usually

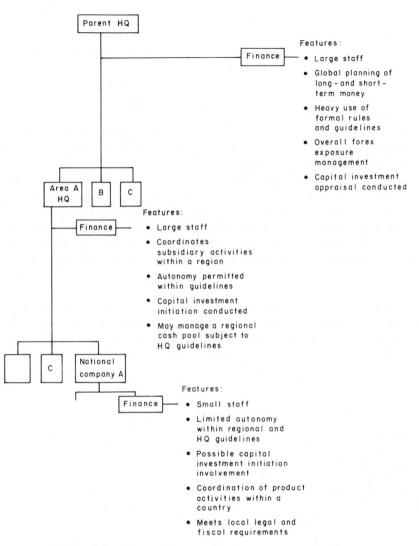

Figure 5.4   Advanced international treasury organization

made at local and regional level. Such organizations require global financial servicing as well as local transaction and lending facilities. An increasing number of major international banks are developing specialist organizational units to service the leading MNCs which enjoy the finest lending rates and require high levels of service sophistication.

5.5 THE BANK CHOICE DECISION

Amongst MNCs from both Europe and the US, the principal decisions about new banks are made at the corporate headquarters. Amongst US MNCs, while the chief financial officer typically decides when to add a bank, the analysis of the decision is usually delegated to a treasurer or assistant treasurer for international banking. European MNCs do not tend to have as well developed a central treasury function and decisions are more likely to be taken by the chief financial officer or a treasurer for international banking. When these questions are asked at the subsidiary level, however, a somewhat less centralized picture emerges. The local subsidiaries of both European and US MNCs claim that bank appointment decisions are shared about equally between headquarters and the subsidiary treasury management. The truth probably lies somewhere between the two, but it is essential if banks wish to gain a substantial share of business at such accounts that a coordinated team marketing effort be developed for each account involving calling both on the central treasury and at major international subsidiaries (and, in particular, regional headquarters units where these exist, as in the advanced treasury management organization). Details of the bank appointment decision process are shown in Table 5.3.

Table 5.3:
How MNCs Make Banking Relationships for their International Operations (%)

Executive responsible	When to add a bank		Which banks to consider		Which bank to select		What balances to maintain	
	US	Euro	US	Euro	US	Euro	US	Euro
Parent co.								
President or chief executive	2	11	1	5	2	9	1	4
Chief financial officer	37	51	17	49	32	47	28	35
Treasurer for int. banking	18	19	16	30	18	25	16	23
Ass. treasurer int.	11	0	25	4	17	0	18	2
Other officer	4	5	7	4	4	7	9	9
Total	72	86	66	92	73	88	72	73
Subsidiary co.								
Chief executive officer	0	9	0	7	0	5	0	5
Senior financial officer	7	9	11	11	8	9	13	7
Financial officer of parent & overseas co. jointly	7	9	11	5	7	11	2	5
Other officer	2	2	1	2	0	2	0	4
Total	16	29	23	25	15	27	16	21

Source: Greenwich Research Associates.

5.6 MIDDLE MARKET TREASURY ORGANIZATION

Because the profit margins available from providing services to large MNCs are so fine, an increasing number of banks are turning their attention to middle market companies where it is expected that loan spreads may be more attractive. Whether this is true or not will remain to be seen. It seems likely that many of these accounts, especially those which are most attractive in terms of growth and the like, will be able to attract very fine rates like the larger multinationals as banks compete for their business. Nevertheless, in servicing these accounts it is important to recognize the differences in their treasury systems by comparison with those of large corporations.

Most middle market companies have a centralized treasury or finance department. This is generally small and similar to the elementary treasury organization, consisting of less than five people in the majority of cases. Many do not have a formal treasury at all, responsibilities resting with the company finance director and some of the accounting staff. In some cases the chief executive is supported only by the accounting function. Thus, as companies get smaller, a less formal approach to treasury management is normal and a small *ad hoc* team of senior company officials tends to deal with finance questions as they arise. These officials are often not financiers or bankers. *It is therefore extremely important to recognize this difference and endeavor to communicate in a language appropriate to the customer and not in banking jargon.*

Most treasury functions in middle market accounts are strongly centralized in terms of where the responsibility for decision-making resides. For most banking services, therefore, it is essential to gain the support and approval of the central office. Calling patterns which emphasize local or even overseas subsidiaries have only a low probability of success. A list of functions which are likely to be strongly controlled at the center and those where decision-making is shared or delegated is given below:

Centralized functions

- Company/group capital structure
- Subsidiary capital structure
- Company/group finance policy
- Subsidiary finance policy
- Company/group cash management
- Company/group working capital
- Company/group tax planning
- Subsidiary tax planning
- Company/group long-term financial planning
- Company/group investment appraisal
- Remittance policy
- Company/group foreign exchange

- Company/group banking relations
- Negotiation of domestic short-term credits
- Negotiation of domestic subsidiary bank relations
- Bank choice for domestic subsidiaries

Shared decisions

- Management of subsidiary foreign exchange
- Subsidiary capital investment
- Subsidiary float
- Domestic subsidiary cash balances
- Global invoicing
- Choice of overseas subsidiary banks
- Negotiation of overseas subsidiary short-term credits
- Negotiation of overseas subsidiary bank relations

Subsidiary-dominated functions

- Management of subsidiary working capital
- Management of invoices
- Stock levels
- Subsidiary bank account
- Overseas subsidiary cash balances

Decentralized functions all relate only to the subsidiary and also generally only apply to short-term financial considerations. Overseas subsidiaries receive slightly more freedom than domestic ones. For bank product design this position suggests that corporate customers might be interested in mechanisms that provide them with better or cheaper control system information to so allow greater decentralization.

The major factors considered by middle market accounts in choosing their lead bank are shown in Table 5.4 for a sample of around 160 such accounts in the UK. The most important factors are the breadth of services offered, the price of loans and an understanding by the bank of the company's needs and problems.

The lower level of interest in international services is immediately apparent in middle market accounts, and this negates one of the key strengths of large international banks. These banks are also less likely to be able to provide the wide service range offered by local banks in overseas countries, are likely to have a higher-cost deposit base which reduces their chance of loan competitiveness, and are less likely to understand local needs than domestic banks. Those international banks wishing to penetrate overseas middle market segments will therefore need to modify their marketing strategies and adjust to the requirements of local middle market accounts if they are to be successful.

Table 5.4:
Factors in the Choice of Principal Bank

	Percentage saying 'very important'
Can provide most services	79
Are price-competitive on loans	76
Understand our needs and problems	70
Are fast on processing transactions	50
Are flexible in tailoring services	50
Are price-competitive on forex	36
Are efficient in international money transfers	29
Are knowledgeable about our industry	20
Have global branch network	21
Knowledgeable about wide range of international services	19
We have used them before	17

Source: Centre for Business Research.

Account officer requirements by middle market accounts are also somewhat different. The main requirements expected of calling officers are shown in Table 5.5.

Table 5.5:
Middle Market Requirements of Bank Calling Officers

	% company mentions	
Prompt and efficient follow-up	93	
Able to convince bank to meet credit needs	71	
Know company's banking needs	60	
Know company's operating structure	53	59*
Make good use of time	53	
Know full range of domestic credit services	50	
Know international banking services	32	50*
Personable	29	
Have detailed industry knowledge	25	
Know non-credit services	23	

*Applies to companies with international subsidiaries.
Source: Centre for Business Research.

The most important factors are the prompt and efficient follow-up of promises made, an ability to convince the *bank* about the customer's credit needs and a proper understanding of what the customer's actual needs are. The second of these reasons is perhaps especially interesting, implying that selling takes place as much within the bank itself as it does to external customers.

5.7 CONCLUSION

It is extremely important to understand the purchasing process at the personal and corporate accounts you are servicing or wish to penetrate in order to improve the chances of marketing success. Check your understanding of your customers and main prospects by asking the following questions:

Corporate banking

1. What is the structure of the customer's treasury function at both central and subsidiary level?
2. Who are the key individuals involved in the purchase decision process?
3. What are their personal motivations?
4. What are the critical motivations for the company in purchasing specific bank services?
5. Are the account needs fully known and understood?
6. Where is the locus of decision-making for each specific service the bank is interested in?
7. Does this knowledge affect the existing account plan strategy, and if so how?
8. Is the bank's market segment strategy appropriate given the customer's purchasing motivations, and if not what charges should be made?

Retail banking

9. Which are the key individual banking account segments that you wish to service?
10. What are the key factors that determine the decision process for each of these?
11. Who are the critical opinion leaders who might influence individual behavior?
12. How can these opinion leaders be best reached and influenced?
13. What specific needs do your actual and potential customers have?
14. How well do your services meet these needs?

CHAPTER 6

Planning corporate account strategy

6.1 INTRODUCTION

The underlying support for market segment/business unit plans in the corporate banking market is the analysis of individual accounts and the preparation of account strategic plans setting out objectives for each account and supplying a strategy to achieve these. The development of such account plans will be a major element in the business unit plan. Account planning will not, however, normally apply to market segments concerned with mass markets such as very small business sectors or normal consumer markets, where the preparation of individual account plans would be impractical. For large corporate and high net worth individual markets, on the other hand, such plans form an essential part of a systematic marketing approach.

The development of account plans provides the market manager with an essential tool for utilizing and monitoring his account officer resources in achieving the overall business unit plan. Account plans fit into the business unit planning structure as shown in Figure 6.1.

6.2 BASIC ACCOUNT SCREENING

From the decision as to what investment strategy should be adopted for each market segment, existing and potential accounts are first screened to identify their basic potential prior to calling.

This initial screening should aim to ensure that adequate potential exists and the account is basically creditworthy. The base data on each account should cover the following:

Basic account data

Financial
— Sales
— Gross margin
— Sales growth rate

97

Figure 6.1

- Net margin
- Margin trend
- Sales percentage by major line of business
- Stocks
- Debtors
- Creditors
- Trends in working capital items
- Plant and equipment
- Property
- Trends in fixed capital investment
- Short-term debt
- Long-term debt
- Debt maturity schedule
- Interest paid
- Times interest covered
- Equity capital
- Major shareholdings

— Net cash flow
— Trends in cash flow
— Detailed ratio analysis
— Trends in ratios
— Credit ratings (e.g. Dun & Bradstreet)

General business
— Lines of business
— Production/service sites (number and location)
— Subsidiaries (domestic and overseas)
— Number of employees
— Market position
— Main brand names
— Names and position of board and financial officers

Industry background information
— Industry economic trends
— Growth rate (historic and projected)
— Capital intensity
— R & D intensity
— Marketing intensity
— Profitability
— Industry competitive environment

Competitor analysis
— Existing lead bankers
— Other bankers

Advisors
— Accountants
— Lawyers
— Consultants used

Review the basic data to ensure that the potential account is consistent with bank exposure and risk requirements and that *an adequate apparent profitable potential exists at the account which might be expected to be open to a competitive approach.* Assuming the potential is evaluated as positive, the account is added to the list of active prospects. This list of prospects will often exceed available calling officer capacity, especially where the bank is operating outside its home country. In this event it is important that the available call capacity is allocated to the best prospects. Bear in mind this will not always mean the largest accounts but rather those where the open market potential is highest. Indeed, many large multinational accounts despite their size are probably now unattractive in profitability terms to most banks. Such accounts are operating in a buyer's market, where there are almost as many banks anxious to provide them with funds and services as there are accounts to be serviced. As a result these large accounts with a high credit standing can command the finest rates for lending and other services.

As a consequence many banks have turned their attention to the 'middle market'. Here too, however, the bank which provides nothing better than an average service will find that competition is intense and profits difficult to achieve. It is important to remember that for banks operating abroad or outside their normal territory most business must be won from indigenous competition by finer rates, superior service or some combination of these two factors. Banks that rely on price alone, however, to win business are unlikely to hold it in the long term unless they can maintain a superior cost of funds position, which will be extremely difficult.

Within each market proposed for expansion as part of the overall bank strategy endeavor to establish an attack order for your accounts for preliminary prospecting. This can usually be achieved by ranking the potential prospects in three or four dimensions drawn from the basic account data such as size, growth rate, capital intensity and competitor lead banks. Having ranked potential prospects, assign these to the available account officers.

6.3 PROSPECTING

After the potential accounts have been screened to identify priority prospects, the second stage of account development is contacting the account with a view to establishing a call program. For those prospects which are priority targets, contact should be made usually with the central finance function. Where this is outside the territory you are planning for, check first that the local subsidiary has autonomy over local bank service choice, and if not clear with account officers in the territory containing the central treasury that your approach is welcome. Don't be discouraged if you are unable to meet with the top finance officer at the first meeting. Indeed, it is often preferable to meet with junior officers initially as the main priority of early meetings is the identification of customer needs, which junior officers may sometimes reveal better than their superiors.

Bear in mind also that at most good corporate accounts you are operating in a buyer's market. The treasuries of most major corporations in developed countries are today almost besieged by a wide array of bankers all seeking to sell their organizations' services. As a result, in many corporate treasuries of major corporations interviewing new banks is delegated to less senior treasury managers. Some companies have even installed a 'bank relationship manager' to shield their line treasury officers. Further, in some countries such as Japan, the status of the calling officer will determine the level of the person seen at the corporate account. Thus one of the tasks in the early stages of account development will be for account officers to identify the structure of the potential client's treasury and recommend an appropriate calling program, making use of tiered calling involving senior bank management as appropriate.

Because of the high cost of account officer time, and despite the initial screening process undertaken, it is still better to try to improve your chances of successful account development by using warm lead contact techniques rather than cold calling. Accounts which do not respond to warm lead techniques can be approached completely cold if it is felt essential, but a failure to respond to such techniques usually indicates the account should be recycled back to the screening data base. Such warm lead techniques include:

1. *Referrals* Generated from a wide variety of sources including bank customers, other banks, bank suppliers, etc.

Many such referrals are random and come without solicitation. Such referrals should be checked first of all by a telephone call to see whether a personal call would be welcome and worthwhile.

Referrals can be actively solicited from all sources. Internal bank cross-selling can be one of the most rewarding business development areas. Most banks study contact lists for other subsidiaries/branches, etc., but carefully designed cross-selling programs are unfortunately rare.

2. *Corporate advertising* Financial service advertising to the corporate market has been growing rapidly.

Most such advertising seems poorly planned and conceived, badly aimed, lacking impact, and unsure about what it is supposed to do.

Advertising, even to the corporate market *can* be useful as a means of lead generation for:

— general image and awareness generation;
— attacking specific segments, e.g. small business, vehicle fleet operators, etc.;
— promoting particular products or services.

Advertising lead generation should be carefully monitored and checked to assess its value:

— check how many responses;
— check changing awareness level;
— check enquiry/conversion ratios;
— check media variation.

3. *Mail shots* Mail shots skim the market and although response levels are low they can be used to identify likely warm prospects.

Many mail shots are seen as 'junk mail' and never reach the person intended. They should therefore appear personalized, not as a bulk production.

Always try to address an individual by name; never just refer to the company.

Mail shots can be very selective in terms of product, customer group, time, geography, etc.

They can be used to spread news quickly.

They can be used to cover market prospects for which the business development executive doesn't have time and as a foil to competitors.

Mail shots should contain news. However, brochures should be used carefully, because if you put too much information in the prospective customer's hands he may decide it's not worth meeting you.

Covering letters should cover no more than one side of paper. Ideally, such a letter should consist of four paragraphs:

   i) State its objective: 'I am writing to invite you to a special meeting of exporters to Eastern Europe at the Grand Hotel on March 8 at 11.30 am with lunch to follow.'

   ii) Show why the topic is relevant: 'This meeting will give details for the first time of our new acceptance credit facilities for Eastern bloc trade and our new money transfer service which speeds money flows from Eastern Europe.'

   iii) Show why the topic is especially interesting to the letter recipient: 'We feel that with your growing trade to Eastern bloc countries these services can help increase your exports and speed up your cash flow from these countries.'

   iv) Restate the objective: 'I hope therefore you will be able to join us at the Grand Hotel on March 8, and I shall telephone you next Thursday to confirm your place at the meeting.'

The mail shot should indicate the action you intend to take. Only in exceptional circumstances or when you know you will get the answer you want should you leave the recipient to take action and reply.

Mail shots should be sent out at a rate at which the necessary follow-up can be handled.

4. *Seminars and demonstrations* All products and services really need to be demonstrated to gain conviction and acceptance — the more difficult the product or service is to demonstrate, the more important it is that a successful demonstration is made.

In banking services, to generate leads, new products and services can usefully be introduced by seminars and demonstrations. Those attending clearly have an interest and a successful demonstration provides prospective customers with a very high probability of conversion.

Relative to the cost of personal calling, seminars and demonstrations are very cheap. If your expertise is really credible they can even become profitable in their own right. Indeed, look actively at charging for seminars in specific subjects: a free seminar will often bring the wrong person whereas a paid-for seminar in a pleasant location may be an excellent opportunity to attract senior treasury managers. The use of existing customers employing the bank's service as speakers at such seminars is particularly useful provided such accounts are themselves appropriate and/or prestigious.

Seminars and demonstrations require considerable effort to set up and professional presentations are important.

Demonstrations at existing customers' premises also add credibility. Prospective customers can see how the product or service works in operational conditions and can talk to your customer about problems and advantages.

5. *Telephone calling* The telephone can be used for many purposes. It is far cheaper than a personal call, enables you to cover substantial numbers of customers quickly, and can be used to substantially improve your probability of business development success. The telephone can be used for:

— setting up appointments for new, follow-up and user calls;
— extending invitations to seminars, demonstrations and social events;
— confirming dates and times of meetings;
— seeking information;
— keeping in touch with existing customers and potential problems.

The telephone is by far the best way of seeking an initial appointment unless the appointment is overseas. If your contact won't talk to you on the 'phone the probability of success is so low that you should either try another contact at a *higher* level in the company or try another company.

Always retain the initiative on the telephone. If your contact is not in, make sure *you* telephone back at a time you know he will be in. If he is in but asks you to call back, try to set a provisional appointment with him which it is his responsibility to break.

Don't give away too much information on the telephone — it offers the customer the opportunity of saying there is no need for you to call.

Make sure you speak to the person you want. Do not be sidetracked by secretaries or telephonists.

The objective of a first telephone call is to arrange a meeting. Offer a benefit, sound interesting and commit him to action.

Keep the initiative in arranging the meeting. If your initial contact is not the decision-maker or key decision influencer get him to give you an introduction and arrange a meeting with the decision-maker.

6.4 NEEDS IDENTIFICATION

When contact with a prospective account has been established the primary purpose of the initial meeting is to begin to try and identify the particular needs of the company and of its financial services decision-makers. Until this is done adequately, selling cannot be undertaken with confidence that a sale will actually satisfy customer needs.

After contact has been made review the preliminary account information base to prepare for your initial meeting. Endeavor to gain an understanding of the prospective account's business activities, the scope of its strategy, the geographic location of subsidiaries and the biographical details of senior officers, in addition to financial and credit details. Where possible also identify which competitor banks provide which services.

The early meetings with the account will be primarily concerned with establishing the size and nature of the account's banking needs. Try to complete the needs/supplier matrix in Figure 6.2. In addition you should aim to gain a detailed understanding of the decision-making structure for buying banking services at the account. When you have performed a detailed needs analysis you should be able to answer the following questions about each account:

Service analysis

— What banking services and in what volume are used by the account?
— What service usages are growing? Stable? Declining?
— Are there any new services presently unused which might meet account needs?

Competitive analysis

— Which banks supply each service and in what volume?
— What is the customer's opinion about the quality of service of each of its bankers?
— What are the strengths and weaknesses of each competitor? Check:
  • Service cover
  • Product quality
  • Price
  • Accuracy
  • Advice
  • Quality of calling officers
  • Legal advantages
  • Personal relationships
— How important is this account to each competitor bank?
— What reaction would each have to a competitive move?

Figure 6.2 Customer needs — competitive position matrix

Customer needs (columns): Local checking accounts, Local deposit services, Local overdraft, Local term loans, Acceptance credits, Export finance, Import finance, Standby LCs, Foreign drafts, Local collections, Local leasing, Local factoring, Cash management services, Treasury advice services, Credit card services, House purchase loans, Investment advice, Trustee services, International currency lending, Loan syndications, International investment advice, Mergers and acquisitions, Foreign trade services, Project finance, Foreign exchange services, Bonds & private placements, Wage payments, Foreign subsidiary finance, International cash management, Buyer credits, Construction loans, Venture capital, Computer services, Machine banking

Supplier		
Bank 1	Volume	
	Trend	
	% share	
Bank 2	Volume	
	Trend	
	% share	
Bank 3	Volume	
	Trend	
	% share	
Bank 4	Volume	
	Trend	
	% share	
This bank	Volume	
	Trend	
	% share	
Total	Volume	
	Trend	
	% share	

— What would be the weakest competitor to move against and with what service?

Decision process

— What is the organization structure of the account's treasury function?
— Where is the basis of decision-making power for each service?
— How loyal is the customer to its bankers?
— How frequently are new banks added or old ones discarded?
— Are there any specific personal needs or whims of treasury officers that we should know about?
— What is the formal and informal power structure of the treasury organization? How can this be best influenced?
— Which services do subsidiary companies/units have any control over?
— How are new bank addition decisions taken?
— What other functions are important in the power structure?
— What are the personal ambitions/aspirations of the key decision-makers?
— How may we best influence these?
— What are the account's future ambitions and what do these mean for long-term financial service requirements? Check:
  • Product strategy
  • Investment policy
  • Mergers and acquisitions
  • Overseas expansion

Bank factors

— What services that the bank offers appear best suited to attack this account?
— Are interest rates and services prices stable enough and profitable enough to be attractive?
— How should we best service this account?
— How many calls should be made by whom and where?
— Is it necessary to set up inter busines unit coordination?
— Is specific industry/service advice required?
— What would be the expected cost of servicing the account?
— What revenue might the bank expect to receive?
— Would the bank be asked to provide loss-making services to penetrate the account?

Your aim should be to demonstrate the competence and reliability of your bank with the expectation that in time you gain the confidence of the account. In this way you will hopefully develop an ultimate lead bank relationship. Do not therefore aim to sell inferior quality services to your customers but rather concentrate on those which are as good as or superior to those of competitors but which are also profitable to your bank.

6.5 ACCOUNT STRATEGY ASSESSMENT

In the same way as deciding on a portfolio of market strategies, account strategies can be determined qualitatively based on account attractiveness and competitive position as shown in Figure 6.3.

Account attractiveness \ Competitive position	High		Low
High	Hold and grow	Penetrate	Improve or withdraw
	Defend strongly	Selective service	Standardized marketing
Low	Maintenance of profitable services	Minimum maintenance	Withdraw

Figure 6.3 Account strategy matrix

Accounts with high account attractiveness and a good competitive position are those for concentrated attention, to be held and grown with concentration paid to cross-selling and cementing a strong existing relationship. High account attractiveness where a moderate account strength exists should be priority targets for increased penetration. Those where the competitive position is high and the attractiveness moderate should be defended vigorously to keep out other competitors. Accounts low in account attractiveness should be maintained for those services which are profitable, and competitors threatening these should be discouraged.

Other account strategies are less positive. Those accounts which are moderately attractive and where a moderate competitive position occurs should be attacked selectively, picking off those services which are especially profitable and where a competitive opportunity exists; low competitive position, high attractiveness accounts should either be attacked vigorously or let go. This will depend in large part on account officer availability. An alternative suggested for moderately attractive accounts with a weak competitive position is to reduce calling needs and cost by offering standardized products or services which can be sold without heavy personal selling support. Low attractiveness accounts with a moderate position should receive only minimum maintenance service so as to reduce the high cost of calling and account support. Finally, accounts with both a low level of attractiveness and low competitive advantage should be abandoned. This tends to be an emotional and difficult decision for many bankers, who often seem to want all the business at every account irrespective of its profitability.

6.6 ACCOUNT ACTION PLANNING

When the appropriate strategic position of your main corporate accounts has been identified, each should be planned accordingly. Where accounts involve several geographic or product-based business units this planning needs to be coordinated and responsibility assigned to an overall account executive, usually the senior officer responsible for servicing the central treasury. This area is often one which can create severe organizational difficulties in many banks due to their existing structures, control systems and reward systems, which lead to problems over internal transfer pricing, the location of credit for transactions booked in a business unit in which the transaction did not occur, and in meeting the needs of accounts in matters such as country limits. By and large, when such difficulties occur it is important to look at the position from the customer's point of view. If the bank is unable to integrate its internal organization and other resources effectively this is a competitive strategic weakness and the customer will so identify it, transferring business to those banks able to provide an integrated service. This problem occurs particularly in geographically organized banks dealing with multisite or multinational clients.

The problem of country limit assessment for large multinational accounts is a common one which some banks find it difficult to resolve. Again, this can be planned when each country-based account officer identifies the account's country limit requirements by currency as part of the annual account planning process. When the account has been identified as one where a growth, defend or penetration strategy is appropriate the planned need can be deducted from the bank's overall country exposure position and effectively allocated to the account. The residual funds are then the responsibility of the geographic business manager charged with optimizing profitability on the free funds allocated to him. Where account demands exceed plan then additional funds need the approval of the bank credit committee, who should bear in mind the potential profit losses at the local country level *versus* the potential overall account profitability gain.

For each account, therefore, the account plan consists of the following:

— Objectives
— Strategy summary sheet

— Action plan description, resource needs, constraints
— Account profitability budget
— Call plan
— Consolidation plan (for multisite accounts)

Account objectives

Using a form such as that shown in Figure 6.4, identify the objectives for the account both short and long term. These should indicate in quantified terms the expected service volume to be achieved, the level of resulting profitability and the market share to be obtained. In addition, a summary strategy statement should be included on how the objective will be achieved. This should identify precisely where other market units or parts of the bank will be involved in this achievement. Finally, specify the dates by when short-term and long-term objectives will be achieved. It is important that the objectives and strategy summary should be sufficiently precise for the result to be clearly and unequivocally measured and progress monitored. All too often plans are written and objectives specified in such general terms that there is virtually no way of assessing whether or not they have been achieved.

Action plans

Using a form such as that shown in Figure 6.5, set out the marketing plan for attacking the account. This form should identify the key account needs established by preliminary calling and account analysis. The needs should be specified in terms of particular service requirements and their estimated priority, the expected volume involved and the level of resulting profitability which might be achieved.

Secondly, the present competitive position should be outlined, indicating realistically the bank's relative strengths and weaknesses compared with the entrenched competition. Where possible an attack should be directed towards a specific competitor, and an indication of what that competitor's strategy is, why yours is superior and what reaction can be expected from such an attack should be included in the action plan.

The plan should also outline the resource needs required to service the marketing strategy. These needs should be indicated in terms of people, including existing account officer calling and any specialist or senior management requirements, any new systems or operations development, specific additional facilities and the level and type of funds required.

Finally, the plan should set out the precise services which you propose to introduce and by when. Indicate how this will be achieved and outline the call program and follow-up strategy you propose to pursue. In the event of a significant under or over achievement of your plan indicate what contingencies you have established to cope with the deviation.

Year: 1983–4
Company: XYZ Corpn SA. Address: Sao Paulo
Parent co.: XYZ Intl Corp. Address: Los Angeles, USA
Main business: Aerospace.   Duns rating:
Strategy position: Penetrate

Market unit: Brazil
Account officer: R. Constanzo
Global acct officer: J. Gordon
Other SBUs involved: Trade finance, project fin.

Account objectives and strategy summary

Product	Account objectives	Strategy summary	Target date
	(Identify target volume, expected profitability and account market share. Indicate both LT & ST objectives)	*(Outline method of achievement. Identify any cooperative efforts with other SBUs)*	*(Specify expected dates for achievement of LT & ST objectives)*
Loans			
Deposits			
FX			
Other fee services			

Figure 6.4   Account planning form 1: objectives

Market unit: Brazil

Customer name: XYZ Corpn SA   Account officer: R. Constanzo

Existing status: SBU prospect _✓_   SBU customer ___   Bank customer ___

Marketing action plan

Key account needs
— Credit services
— FX
— Cash management
— Trade finance

(Identify key account needs in terms of priority, volume, profitability)

Bank competitive position
— Strengths
— Weaknesses
— Competitor strategy
— Competitor reaction

(Identify bank's relative strengths and weaknesses relative to entrenched competition. Where competitive displacement is expected, indicate which competitor, what that bank's strategy is, and what reaction should be expected)

Resource needs
— People
— Systems
— Facilities
— Funds

(Identify precise resource needs and dates by which they would be required)

Marketing strategy
Services to introduce
Mode of introduction
Support services required
Call programme required
Follow-up strategy anticipated
Contingency plans

(Identify precise services to be introduced and by when. Indicate how this will be achieved, what support services will be expected from other units within the SBU and the bank. Outline expected call programme and follow-up strategy. Specify contingency plans)

Figure 6.5   Account planning form 2: action plans

Account profitability budget

The profitability expected from the account should be budgeted using a form similar to that shown in Figure 6.6. In addition the management control system should produce a regular printout of performance against budget together with a variance report for under and over performance of more than 10 per cent. In some banks this type of system produces monthly reports while in others account printouts are prepared quarterly. Such a system provides a vital control and monitoring service which can also be used to check product, geography and industry performance as required right down to the level of the individual account officer. As a result changes can be made in strategy and/or expected outcomes through early control system signals rather than finding

Customer Name:
Account profitability budget 19

Market Unit
Account officer

	Q1 REV/ Vol. Rate EXP	Q2 REV/ Vol. Rate EXP	Q3 REV/ Vol. Rate EXP	Q4 REV/ Vol. Rate EXP	Total 198 REV/ Vol. Rate EXP	Previous year REV/ Vol. Rate EXP
Local currency						
Short-term credits						
Medium-term credits						
Other credit products						
Loan related fees						
Non-interest bearing deposits						
Interest bearing deposits						
Local net funds revenue						
Foreign currency						
Short-term credits						
Medium-term credits						
Other credit products						
Loan related fees						
Non-interest bearing deposits						
Interest bearing deposits						
Foreign net funds revenue						
Total net funds revenue						
Foreign exchange revenue						
Cash management fees						
Other non-funded revenue						
Credit losses						
Cost of servicing						
Net profit						

Figure 6.6   Account profitability budget form

performance is different from budget when it is too late to take corrective action.

6.7 CALL PLAN DEVELOPMENT

The cost of making bank personal calls is expensive both in terms of actual cost and in account officer time. The call intensities of leading banks vary widely and this is a primary mechanism for bank differentiation. For large multinationals some banks employ very intense calling, where the account officer or 'relationship manager' might look after as few as four or five accounts. Such an individual is trained as a generalist rather than as a lending banker and acts as the principal contact for most bank services making use of specialists or senior management calls as required. These officers may also enjoy significant seniority, being paid the equivalent of relatively senior management grades. In addition they may also possess a substantial lending discretion so that they can negotiate from a position of seeming equality with the corporate treasurer. Where the size of the financial requirements of the account is beyond his normal lending capacity, the relationship manager can still be allowed to negotiate within predetermined limits established by the bank's central lending committee or its equivalent. Such officers may also visit the account around the world as required while making use of local calling officers for day-to-day subsidiary company contact.

The global account officer (GAO) concept is a variant of this system. In banks using this form of organization it is common that an officer has global responsibility for two or three accounts and also serves in a local account officer role for another seven or so. The GAO is then usually responsible for a worldwide team of officers all calling on units of the multinational client. Each local officer prepares his own account plan which is in turn consolidated by the GAO before final management approval or rejection. A large multinational can thus be serviced by up to 20 or 30 local officers, or the equivalent of some three full-time officers servicing the one account. Given the high cost of such officers the level of business needing to be generated to ensure the account is profitable to the bank is obviously substantial, especially in view of the fine spreads such accounts command.

Other banks operate less intensive calling systems or ones which are less coordinated. Banks such as those in Western Europe tend to appoint a senior manager as a global account officer, but this is often for a large number of accounts. Alternatively, such officers are not employed full-time to deal with these accounts, being perhaps principally responsible for other bank activities. Further, these banks rarely coordinate their officers' activities around the world. They are therefore less able to provide an intensive level of calling and hence may find it more difficult to develop a close working relationship with the treasury managers. By comparison, those banks offering an intensive calling program aim to develop the position of their relationship managers into that of a confidant or advisor to the central treasury.

Call intensity also varies significantly with size. For middle market accounts banks vary their account loadings from around 15 to 60 accounts per officer. Again wide variations occur, with European banks in general tending to give less intensive call cover than North American banks.

No precise rules, therefore, apply to establishing call patterns. For each account the call strategy should be determined on the following basis:

— Bank policy and organization
— Account decision-making process
— Account organization and site location
— Account financial requirements
— Bank resource availability
— Account potential
— Competitive bank practice

By and large the policy of one call a year to review existing overdraft arrangements is unsatisfactory for building a close relationship, and for grow, defend or penetrate strategy accounts a minimum call value of four per annum would be reasonable. For large accounts requiring a substantial range of bank services call intensity should obviusly be greater and involve different tiers of the bank's management in order to broaden the personal base of the account relationship. This is in addition to the use of specialists for relevant services such as foreign exchange or cash management. In setting your call strategy, therefore, plan, using a form similar to that in Figure 6.7, for the following factors:

— Number of calls
— Timing of calls
— Who to contact
— Who to make the call

Each time a call is made it should then be reported using a form similar to that shown in Figure 6.8. Firstly, the call objectives should be specified to indicate what it was you expected to achieve. Secondly, details should be provided of who was present and what was discussed, together with any action which was required. Such initiatives should always involve the bank rather than relying upon the customer to take action if positive selling techniques have been used. Further, a successful close should always aim to commit the customer to at least an incremental step towards your account objective

6.8 CONSOLIDATION PLANS

For those accounts serviced by a number of calling officers and involving multiple sites usually in a variety of countries an integrated marketing strategy

115

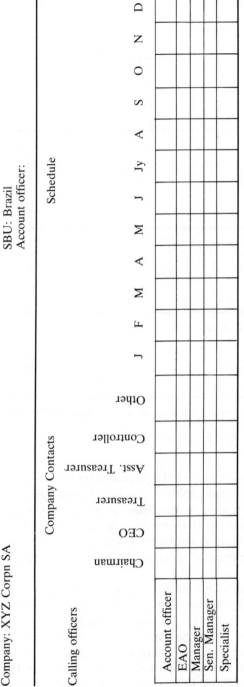

Figure 6.7 Account planning form 3: call program

Company Name: _____   Account officer: _____
Interviewed: _____   date: _____
_____   Date of last call: _____
_____

Call objective:

Topics discussed in detail:

Other topics discussed:

Discussion summary:

Follow-up required by account Officer:

       By others:

Other information, e.g. competitive activities, business activity, etc.

Figure 6.8   Call report form

is required so as to achieve the full potential of the resources committed by the bank to service the account. Where this is not done local branches may, for example, attempt in vain to penetrate at account subsidiaries where the ultimate responsibility for changing bank relationships is held by the central treasury. Similarly, using a GAO concept without providing the GAO with the necessary account management responsibility makes this task unnecessarily difficult.

A consolidation plan for such accounts should therefore be prepared by the GAO which brings together the individual country/market unit account plans. This consolidated plan should indicate the global expected commitments of resources by country and by currency, and the expected returns together with a breakdown of precisely where specific commitments will actually be made and by whom. In this way account trade-offs can be examined and decisions taken so as to maximize the general profitability of the account. For

Company Name:
Global account profitability report, month, year

Market:
Global account officer:

	Parent company			Overseas subsidiary			Overseas subsidiary			Overseas subsidiary			Overseas subsidiary			Total account	
	Actual	Budget	Variance	Actual	Budget	Variance	Actual	Budget	Variance	Actual	Budget	Variance	Actual	Budget	Variance	Actual	Budget
Loan demand ($)																	
Loan demand local																	
Deposits ($)																	
Deposits local																	
Net funds revenue																	
Loan fees																	
FX commission																	
Cash management																	
Collections																	
Other fee income																	
Net revenue																	
Cost of services																	
Account profitability																	
Account ROA																	

Figure 6.9 Global account profitability report form

example, an acceptance of, say, poor sovereign risk lending in one country which leads to a loss can be accepted if at the same time a compensatory arrangement can be made elsewhere such that the overall level of return is satisfactory. Overall responsibility for global account plan achievement rests with the GAO, with each local unit account officer being responsible for the component under his or her control. In a similar way the bank's control system should report on consolidated account performance at regular intervals using a form similar to that shown in Figure 6.9.

6.9 SUMMARY

Account analysis and marketing planning is an important method of systematically attacking your key accounts and an essential component in wholesale banking market strategy. From the strategic decision of what markets you intend to adopt particular strategies in, account planning involves a six-stage process. Firstly, an account data base should be built which can be interrogated in order to identify account potential and so determine whether the account is worth actively soliciting. For those accounts seen as being attractive to call on, active prospecting begins with an attempt to contact the account with a view to establishing a call program. Initial contact should be made using warm lead techniques where possible. The primary purpose of early calls should be to clearly establish account needs, the decision process for purchasing banking services and needs, the decision process for purchasing banking services and the existing structure of competition at the account. This information established, the account can be classified and assigned to an appropriate marketing strategy. Once this has been done detailed account marketing plans are drawn up which identify the objectives set for the account and the action plans for achieving them. This stage also includes a budget of services to be used and the expected profitability. In addition, where appropriate, consolidation plans are prepared for accounts involving several bank business units. Call plans are also established for each account consistent with bank resources policy and the nature and complexity of the individual account needs.

6.10 ACCOUNT PLANNING CHECKLIST

In evaluating account plans check that the plan is satisfactory by asking the following questions:

Screening and prospecting

1. Are the basic account data sufficient to judge the account? If not, what additional information is required and where can it be obtained?
2. Is the review of account potential realistic?

3. Does the potential meet the bank's criteria for profitability and risk?
4. Has the account been correctly ranked as to its priority for development consistent with overall bank strategy?
5. Has the account been allocated to an account officer with adequate time to undertake business development?

Needs identification

6. Are the account needs clearly defined?
7. Are the account's present banking service requirements identified by volume? Price? Usage pattern?
8. Has the position of existing and potential competitors been clearly identified?
9. Have the competitor strengths and weaknesses been analysed relative to the bank?
10. Are these assessments realistic?
11. Have potential competitor reactions been assessed and the weakest competitors identified?
12. Is the decision process clearly understood at both corporate and subsidiary level and the locus of power for major service identified?
13. Is the formal and informal organization of the account treasury known and the key individuals identified together with their needs, personalities and what influences them?
14. Are the future intentions of the account specified and the long-term financial service implications identified?
15. Have the appropriate bank services to penetrate the account been specified together with expectations on price and profitability?
16. Has a strategy been identified on how to approach the account together with estimates of resource requirements and the expected financial returns?

Strategy assessment

17. Has the appropriate strategic category for the account been specified and is this accurate?
18. Is the strategy category consistent with the bank's strategy assessment for this market?

Action planning

19. Is the action plan drawn up for the account complete and does it sound feasible?
20. Are the short-term and long-term moves suggested appropriate to the account strategy?

21. Are the account objectives specified in a measurable form with clear milestones as to when they will be achieved?
22. Are the resources identified as necessary to implement the proposed account strategy realistic and available?
23. Are any critical constraints identified and if so are measures indicated on how to overcome these?
24. Has the account profitability budget been prepared and is it realistic?
25. Has an appropriate call plan been specified and can this be met from existing officer and management resources?
26. Are areas for interunit coordination identified and steps proposed to ensure that adequate integration actually occurs?
27. Has a global account plan been developed if appropriate and do all concerned know and accept their role in its implementation?
28. Have contingency plans been developed in the event of over or under achievement and are these plans realistic?

CHAPTER 7

Product Range and Development Strategy

7.1 PRODUCT RANGE

Corporate bankers today offer an ever-increasing range of products and services. The traditional lines of demarcation which existed between types of banks such as those between commercial banks and merchant banks have gradually disappeared so that today most international banks will offer a service range covering most aspects of banking and related financial services. However:

— banks are *not* all the same in their skill at delivering particular services;
— banks do not organize to offer similar services in similar ways;
— may banks specialize in particular services in which they will have a distinctive competence relative to their competitors;
— most banks service the corporate market *without* adequately integrating their own organizational capability, resulting in multiple calling and individual bankers having only limited knowledge about their own bank's service range;
— many bank's product manuals are overcomplex and do not act as a marketing guide to the account officers responsible for servicing individual accounts;
— many calling officers who are allegedly generalist bankers are weak in product knowledge, especially of non-credit services.

The most important basic services offered by a bank are the generation of deposits and the subsequent lending of these for interest. The majority of bank profitability is presently still obtained from the interest differential between these services. However, there are many specific forms or alternative products which can be generated within these basic services. It is largely the way that individual banks can develop specially tailored lending and deposit-generating products that enables them to differentiate themselves from competitors and to build market share within specific market segments.

121

7.2 DEPOSIT SERVICES

The range of deposit services which might be found includes:

— Current accounts
— Savings accounts
— Term deposit accounts
— Treasury certificate accounts
— Bank certificates of deposit
— Foreign currency hold accounts
— Collections and float (cheques, notes, money drafts, trade accept-
ances, letters of credit)
— Interbank deposits

Personal deposits have traditionally been the main source of bank funds. These were collected as savings and also constituted the balance on current or checking accounts. It was a popular misconception that such current account credit balances constituted a 'free' resource to large commercial banks. This is not so, the real cost of such deposits being around 6–8 per cent dependent upon the efficiency of individual banks in servicing such accounts. In many countries these accounts are now being forced to pay interest as consumers become more sophisticated and competition for deposits develops.

In the UK, the share of personal deposits held by the major banks has been subject to a steady decline in the postwar period due largely to the attack of building societies, so that today banks are increasingly dependent upon the interbank market and other wholesale deposit sources, notably the eurocurrency markets, as sources of funds. This trend, together with intensified global competition between banks, has sharply reduced the spreads between deposits and lending. Banks have still not been forced to pay money market interest rates on current account balances nor do they voluntarily offer sweep facilities between savings and current accounts.

In the United States, by contrast, banks have been forced to pay competitive rates for virtually all forms of consumer deposits. In the late 1970s, seizing on the interest rate ceiling of around 5 per cent imposed on banks by Regulation Q, brokerage houses offered an alternative service, packaging small parcels of retail deposits into large money market funds which were mainly invested in bank certificates of deposit at current money market wholesale rates. During the inflationary early 1980s the gap between wholesale rates and bank deposit rates widened dramatically, with the result that banks suffered a severe loss of retail deposits as money market funds grew.

From 1981 US banks were allowed to offer interest-bearing checking accounts, NOW accounts, although these were still restricted to 5.25 per cent interest. To stem the flow of deposits, banks moved to sell their own certificates of deposit direct but it was not until early 1983 that they were able to offer competitive interest rates on savings deposits. These new accounts, dubbed Supernow accounts, tended to offer two-tier interest rate facilities. The first $1500 or so of the account balance paid 5.25 per cent interest plus charges for individual transactions. Balances above this level paid a rate close to prevailing money market levels. The introduction of such accounts, while a competitive necessity, significantly increased the average cost of funds of those banks, traditionally heavily dependent on retail deposits, such as Wells Fargo or Bank of America. Nevertheless, the introduction of Supernow's has helped to reverse the flow of funds to low cost delivery system brokerage houses.

The critical segments for retail deposit gathering have become the high and medium net worth individual market accounts. For such individuals, originally highlighted by the Merrill Lynch Cash Management Account, more and more banks have begun to offer superior services, including automatic credit lines, brokerage, investment management services and the like as well as money market interest rates on deposits. Specialist private banking units have also been established by many banks, usually in low tax areas, to provide an additional level of service for very wealthy private depositors.

As a result of the rising cost of retail deposits, the basic *raison d'être* of conventional branches has come into question. Traditionally, conveniently sited to collect personal savings as well as provide ease of access for withdrawals, bank branches in the mid-1980s look an increasingly expensive way of collecting such deposits and delivering banking services. Further, new delivery systems make it less likely that individuals as well as corporations need visit a physical branch. Banks without such expensive branch structures are therefore finding that they are not significantly disadvantaged in raising their deposits in the wholesale market, while those with many branches are forced to examine carefully their operating cost structures.

Deposit-generating products and the whole area of liabilities management have tended to be neglected by banks. In the 1980s deposit generation and the design of a wider, more selective range of liability products is likely to be much more important. Many such products are likely to try to lock in deposits for longer periods, while short-term liabilities management will become more critical as banks tend to lose both corporate float and consumer savings and chequing account deposits. Overall, the cost of funds can be expected to rise to around money market rates.

7.3 LENDING AND CREDIT SERVICES

Lending has traditionally been the most important single banking function and the principal source of revenue. The range of lending and credit services is extremely extensive, perhaps the most important single area of banking activity, and includes:

— Overdraft

- — Fixed-rate short term
- — Acceptance finance
- — Multicurrency lending
- — Term loans
- — Commodity and stock loans
- — Accounts variable loans and factoring
- — Industrial sales finance (secured equipment loans)
- — Merchanting loans
- — Parallel loans
- — Multicurrency credits
- — Import finance
- — Leverage leasing
- — Tax leasing
- — Sale and leaseback
- — Hire purchase
- — Project finance
- — ECGD finance
- — Eurocurrency loans
- — Syndicated loans
- — Fixed rate Eurobonds
- — Floating rate Euromarket notes
- — Retail instalment financing for dealers
- — Property construction loans
- — Merger and acquisition finance
- — Mortgage finance
- — Currency and interest rate swap loans

7.3.1 Usage of Lending and Credit Services by Multinational Corporate Accounts

A recent survey of international credit services used by a sample of 505 US and European MNCs revealed some variations between the enterprises of the two continents in terms of the range of services most used. See facing page.

Amongst US MNCs the services most rapidly increasing in use are private placements overseas, project financing, parallel loans and long-term Eurocurrency bond issues. In addition, some one-third of US MNCs had added a new bank for one or more international credit services in the past year.

The pattern of service usage was somewhat different for European MNCs. American MNCs used performance letters of credit more frequently than European MNCs, which in turn made more use of medium-term export finance, import financing, US domestic loans for investments, Eurocurrency lines of credit and project financing. In addition, the fastest growing services in European MNCs were medium-term export financing, project financing and loans abroad for foreign investments. Like the American MNCs, more than a

How Use of International Credit Services Varies among MNCs (%)

Credit service	US MNCs	European MNCs
Performance letters of credit	58	42
Eurocurrency lines of credit	43	54
Eurocurrency medium-term loans	33	33
Multicurrency lines of credit	32	N/A
Project financing	21	31
Parallel loans	21	N/A
Short-term export finance	N/A	44
Medium-term export finance	18	36
Import financing	14	28
US loans for foreign investments	13	24
Foreign loans for foreign investments	N/A	54
Eurocurrency long-term bond issues	11	N/A
Export letters of credit	N/A	62
Multicurrency borrowing advice	N/A	50
Private placement of equity or debt overseas	9	N/A

Source: Greenwich Research Associates.

third of the companies had added a bank for an international credit service during the past year.

The list of lending products is long and many others exist. However, a number of factors should be borne in mind regarding these:

— Money can be borrowed at fixed and floating rates.
— Loans may be secured against specific assets—this is common practice in specialist lending areas such as shipping and construction.
— Loans may be unsecured—this is normal practice in the non-specialist corporate market.
— Loans may be guaranteed—this is common where the borrower is part of a group of companies. Guarantees can vary from a full guarantee to lesser commitments such as letters of support, or guarantees against part of a project, etc.
— Loans may be in one currency or in a variety of currencies. The exposure risk can be offset or carried by the borrower.
— Loans may be repayable on demand or committed to the borrower for a specific term.
— Term commitments may be for:
  • short or long term;
  • fixed or floating interest rate;
  • repayment may be amortised over the life of the loan or as full amount at the end of the loan;
  • facilities can be revolving.

The traditional pattern of UK commercial bank lending has been to use overdraft. In theory, such money is effectively available at call and security is taken as a charge against specific assets or as a floating charge against all assets. The evaluation of risk in such cases has tended to be mainly by historic balance sheet evaluation on a 'gone' basis. Overdraft lending is designed largely to meet short-term working capital need fluctuations. However, many banks use this form of lending to cover most of the lending needs of corporate clients. This tends to be unimaginative in that it does not attempt to tailor lending products to customer needs and inefficient in that take-up rates of overdraft facilities are only around 60 per cent on average.

The introduction of American banking techniques has led to the widespread adoption of term lending practices. Loans are made usually unsecured, carry a slightly higher rate than overdraft and run for periods of 3–10 years (depending upon specific company situations and market conditions). Such loans can be better tailored to company needs and arranged to meet cash flow and similar requirements. They are useful for covering hard-core debt or financing specific term related projects. They are relatively efficient in that they are normally wholly taken up. Credit assessment for such loans requires the analysis of the *future* position of a company and relies much more on future cash flow analysis. Standard US banking practice usually demands regular financial reviews with the company to whom a facility has been granted and the adoption of a loan document incorporating carefully developed covenants which act as a discipline on corporate management.

Such financial disciplines are less used by European commercial bankers, and as a result term lending, while being increasingly adopted, has often been undertaken *without* adequate financial analysis, careful assessment of covenants and the provision of adequate ongoing financial information.

A detailed understanding of forward financial projection credit assessment procedures and the strategic analysis of potential accounts together with an ability to evaluate the ongoing business as well as financial position of a loan account are considered to be important ingredients in corporate banking product knowledge irrespective of the type of loan under consideration.

Increasingly important alternatives to straightforward lending are also emerging, in particular, perhaps notes and bonds, which are a significant medium-term loan alternative.

In the mid 1980s the market for lending has changed dramatically. Instead of making loans to carry on their own book, banks have 'securitized' them by converting loans into notes or bonds which can be traded in secondary markets. Floating Rate Notes (FRNs) and Note Issuing Facilities (NIFs) have become especially popular with corporations and credit worthy governments. Banks have also actively packaged and 'sold' loan participations to other banks although this has still not developed into a formal secondary market. This trend to disintermediation was being forced on banks as their cost of funds has increased and even become higher than that of some of their customers. It has also enabled banks to reduce their balance sheet exposure. For the commercial banks this trend was leading them to strengthen their merchant or investment banking groups and to run down their traditional lending activities.

Bankers need to understand about such products in order to recommend the most appropriate service. Unfortunately, many bank executives have poor product knowledge of service ranges immediately outside those offered by the bank component of a related financial services corporation such as most major banks now are.

Not all loan services are normally offered by one section of the bank. Large term lending, currency loans and the like are often handled by international or merchant banking divisions, while credit finance, leasing and specialist loans may well be made by specialist subsidiaries.

7.3.2 Retail Lending Areas

Despite higher loan loss rates than with corporate accounts, banks in the mid-1980s have returned to increasing their lending to the retail market. This segment offers the opportunity for high spreads which if the loans are written with low cost offer significant profit opportunities. At the bottom end of the market, therefore, such loans are largely becoming automated, with credit scoring and electronic card delivery systems. This applies in credit card operations, retail revolving credit and the smaller levels of individual credit finance. For upmarket consumers automatic credit lines can be triggered against holdings of securities, bank certificates of deposit and the equity content of home ownership. Mortgage finance is also becoming recognized as an especially attractive product for delivering credit services. Thus while first mortgage finance tends to be provided at a relatively low cost, it is not only secured against the value of property but offers the opportunity to sell insurance services, home improvement loans, real estate brokerage and the like. Further, the mortgage customer base usually remains 'loyal' during the period of home occupancy.

7.3.3 High Growth and Specialist Lending Areas

In the 1980s specialist lending products will probably take on increasing importance as banks strive for improved profitability by concentrating on niches which offer better returns. Key areas for specialization include the following:

Sovereign Risk

In the mid-1980s sovereign risk lending had become an area of major difficulty as a growing number of developing economies loomed close to default. Forced to borrow to finance energy deficiencies and to fund economic growth, many countries took advantage of the Eurocurrency markets' recycling of oil-producing country trade surpluses. Having placed their surpluses with Western banks, the oil producers' funds were recycled to the developing economies, building a sovereign risk loan portfolio which had grown to a massive $800b by 1984. Unable to pay these sums back, the developing economies were forced to seek rescheduling agreements which rolled up not only the repayments of principal but also of interest, causing a potentially massive problem for the leading Western private banks. As a result, sovereign risk lending, while still important, was an area which banks were extremely reluctant to increase unless coupled with adequate guarantees.

Real Estate.

For some large commercial US banks real estate lending constitutes around 25 per cent of the loan portfolio. This usually consists of a combination of activities some of which are more profitable than others. Fixed mortgage lending is a poor area for lending in times of high interest variation and many US banks have significant portions of their portfolios locked in at low rates for mortgage finance. Variable rate or medium-term bullet loans are an alternative which reduces the risk of such lending. In specific segments first mortgage lending can thus be relatively attractive.

The second mortgage market for home improvement/personal spending is also attractive since interest rates are closer to credit finance rates and still involve the security of personal property. Commercial real estate lending tends to be mainly short and medium term, covering construction finance, although some long-term mortgage finance may be attractive, especially if it can be designed to incorporate elements of capital gain. Banks have been periodically caught by fluctuating real estate values, particularly when rising markets fall sharply for a period. However, good spreads are achievable given a sufficient core of expertise. Those banks successful in commercial real estate lending are likely to have a full core of specialists including construction engineers, valuers, progress inspectors, and the like. Further, they will be focused on particular geographic areas and/or industrial sectors such as shopping center complexes. Geographic markets such as South Florida, Texas and Southern California in the US have constituted such high growth areas, offering excellent lending and profit opportunity for the knowledgeable bank but also serious potential pitfalls for the unwary.

Energy

Like real estate, energy is a high potential sector presenting good opportunities (including capital gains) for knowledgeable bankers offering creative financing packages. The most attractive opportunities are likely to be in particular segments of the energy market, such as large projects which require both long-term and interim construction finance as well as forex, and in intermediate sized energy companies, where collateral may well consist of oil in the ground or the like. Again direct equity participation (where permitted) may be attractive or cash flow financing may provide a similar opportunity for non-interest profits. In energy, as in real estate, superior ROAs can be achieved by banks with expertise. Some US banks, notably those based in areas such as Texas, have high energy elements in their loan protfolio and specialize in lending to independent operators rather than large MNC oil companies. Such banks carry a full staff of energy specialists including petroleum engineers, geologists and the like capable of evaluating oil or other energy deposit potential. Banks unable to provide such expertise should not engage in speculative investment because risks can be high without adequate knowledge. The recent disaster of Penn Square is a timely reminder of how a lack of adequate loan evaluation can end in disaster.

Minerals and Mining

This is closely related to energy and project finance and the same rules tend to apply. Such lending, however, may be more international in its make up and potentially vulnerable to sovereign risk; this, while true in oil, can be constrained there by the choice of geographic areas of concentration.

Trade Finance

Long an attractive area for bankers, trade finance still offers potential opportunities of above-average prospect. In particular, the potential development of more interventionist roles by the banker in stimulating all elements of a trade finance chain may well offer high growth. Japanese commercial banks, which are usually part of a highly diversified industrial group which also contains a major trading company, offer a prime example of an integrated organizational model which many Western banks would do well to take note of. Successful banks concerned with trade finance will also require adequate knowledge of the geographic areas in which they wish to specialize, e.g. South-east Bancorp in the Caribbean Basin, Hong Kong and Shanghai covering the Pacific Rim. In addition, good operations processing skills are important.

The area of trade finance, however, may develop into one which presents future dangers for the banking industry. Many banks and non-banks are creating international trading companies similar in concept to the Japanese Soga Shosha but clearly lacking the latter's depth of product, communications and trading experience. Moreover a growing element of such trading is likely to be in the form of counter or barter trading, since many developing economies are already at or beyond prudent country limit exposures. In practice, counter trade and barter also represent a variant of sovereign lending coupled with commodity futures, and considerable care will be needed if banks stake exposed positions in countertrade to ensure future difficulties do not occur.

Correspondent Banking

This is an area which has tended to be neglected in the past and has now reemerged as fashionable. While lending *per se* is not seen as a primary product, the provision of correspondent banking financial services in a variety of areas from operations, transactions and correspondent provisions to joint venture lending is all of potential interest for large commercial banks. Again, specialization to identify service needs and provide service quality is the key to success.

Project Finance

Often treated somewhat differently to conventional lending, project finance is positioned within the merchant banking units of many banks rather than forming a part of line lending operations. As a merchant banking activity, project finance may require the managed syndication of large loans often involving sovereign risk. For the bank such a loan will usually carry a coupon spread plus management fee. However, many projects actually also require the involvement of line lending officers since such investments could involve participants from many industries and countries. Creative financing opportunities which may well require significant line lending and merchant banking integration are therefore keys to success, together with competent specialist project appraisal skills.

Credit Finance

The area of credit finance has been seen as attractive by many banks. A variety of products exist under this general heading for both consumer and corporate markets. Credit finance products usually cover medium-term loans and are supported by the value of the article which is being financed. Generally, rate structures are significantly higher than with conventional loans, although administrative costs together with risk are also higher, both due to default and mistakes in the calculation of residual values.

Credit finance has traditionally been treated by most banks as a separate business. It is also seen by many bankers as different and of lower status. As a consequence, most banks manage their credit finance subsidiaries (many of which were independent before being acquired and added to bank business portfolios in recent years) *via* a separate organization. This often means suboptimal performance by banks who do not maximize any synergy that may exist with other banking products. A recent trend has been the development of global credit finance businesses, notably in consumer lending.

Leasing

Leasing has been an area of significant growth for banks in recent years. It usually offers a customer a lower interest rate when the leasee is unable to use the investment tax benefits normally available for capital investment. These are taken by the lessor and passed back to some extent in the form of a lower interest rate. However, leasing usually provides the bank with a superior rate of return to that obtained on conventional lending.

Leasing is potentially a form of lending which offers substantial opportunities for creative financing to tailor the final product to the customer's need. It also effectively provides a tax shield to bank earnings. Cross-border leasing may be expected to continue to grow substantially and for large ticket items banks will be able to continue to develop the business by moving to leveraged leasing if and when internal profitability or balance sheet constraints make the use of internal funds undesirable.

Like credit finance, leasing still tends to be organized separately from conventional banking activities. As an activity it developed in a similar manner to credit finance and outside mainstream banking. In practice, however, leasing clearly represents an alternative to conventional term lending and its fundamentals need to be clearly understood by lending bankers. There are some signs that in future leasing in particular may be integrated with banking services and, while specialist officers may be used to develop creative leasing contracts, the service may be actively sold by relationship officers.

Notes and Bonds

The securitization of corporate lending has led to substantial growth in the volume of money raised in the form of tradeable instruments. In the United States a variety of commercial paper based products have developed and in the Euromarkets a growing profusion of new, flexible instruments have been produced since the early 1980s.

The growth in tradeable securities, rather than syndicated loans, has accelerated the trend of commercial banks to build their investment banking capabilities. Historically the main competitors in the bond markets had been the major US investment banks and major brokerage houses, and commercial banks were actively trying to break in to this sector via the use of acquisitions and the addition of a new generation of generalist bankers.

Swaps and Futures

New forms of creative finance which have emerged in the past few years and which are growing rapidly are interest rate and currency swaps and the provision of medium- and long-term funds *via* the financial futures market.

Venture Capital

A number of banks have begun to take a very active interest in venture capital situations, for many years a neglected product in the banking industry. In many of the leading Japanese and US banks specialist units have been established to provide advice, consultancy and finance to venture corporations, especially those engaged in high technology areas. In return the banks have taken significant equity positions which it is hoped will ultimately produce substantial capital profits.

Middle Market

The key corporate market segment for competitive attack in the mid-1980s has become the 'middle market'. Loosely defined in most banks as organizations with turnovers of between $10 and £150m per annum, many banks are beginning to carefully segment this group of companies and endeavor to offer their less sophisticated treasury functions a range of asset- and fee-based services.

7.4 OTHER SERVICES

In addition to lending and deposit products, banks also provide a range of other general and specialist services which are usually fee-generating or provided free or highly subsidized to customers making use of other revenue-producing services. These services would include:

1. *General banking services*
   — Domestic transfers
     - Cheques
     - Credit transfers
     - Standing orders
     - Bank-to-bank transfers
     - Direct debits
     - Banker payments
     - EFT transfers
     - Lock boxes

   — International transfers
     - Mail transfers
     - EFT transfers
     - Bank draft
     - Customers' cheques

— Commercial credits
  - Clean credits
  - Documentary credits
  - Import and export credits

— Foreign exchange services

2. *Specialist services*

— Consultancy services
  - Money management
  - Invoicing centers
  - Treasury management services
  - Pension fund management advice
  - Insurance management advice
  - Foreign exchange rate forecasting
  - Banking and financial education

— Trust services
  - Stock and bond purchases
  - Executorships
  - Trusteeships
  - Pension fund management
  - Life insurance
  - Corporate trustee services
  - Stock registrars
  - Dividend payments
  - Investment portfolio advice and management
  - Safety deposit services
  - Estate planning
  - Tax planning

— Other services
  - Payroll management and acountin₅
  - Data processing services
  - Factoring
  - Travel arrangements
  - Correspondent banking services
  - Non-life insurance
  - Life insurance
  - Economic study services
  - Consumer banking services

7.4.1 The Growing Importance of Fee-Based Services

The range of non-lending and credit services offered by banks is becoming increasingly large as the organizations become more diversified. Banks are also now placing greater emphasis on the provision of specialist services, especially for the corporate market, as a means of generating fee income (such services, unlike loans, do not require counterbalanced deposits, and thus supporting additional equity finance), to establish credibility as a bank with specialist skills, to gain an initial entry to corporate accounts (payroll and foreign exchange are two well-used services for this purpose) and to achieve a distinctive competence. In particular, a wide variety of electronic banking services including information processing are becoming of great significance.

One particular problem which must be understood is the use of cross-subsidization. Many bank services are offered free as a courtesy, the cost being borne by income-generating activities. There will be increasing pressure to *unbundle* these courtesy services and to let them reflect their true economic cost. Many corporate treasurers are also keen to unbundle bank services so that customers only pay for services used, rather than being charged for those which are really unnecessary.

Nevertheless, non-credit services play an important role in establishing corporate banking relationships, which in turn normally lead to the development of future lending business. Amongst multinationals the most widely used non-credit services are:

Most companies make use of foreign exchange services and international money transfers, and amongst US MNCs, for the nearly one-third of companies which had added a bank during the past year foreign exchange advice had been the most common single reason. The most rapidly growing international service for US MNCs, however, in both absolute and relative terms was international cash management services. Amongst European MNCs there was a slightly lower tendency for companies to add banks for internation-

Use of International Non-Credit Services Amongst MNCs (%)

Non-credit services	US MNCs	European MNCs
Forex trading and advisory services	78	N/A
International money transfers	78	81
Foreign economic advice	58	44
Documentary collections	56	76
Foreign credit investigations	45	N/A
International cash management services	43	N/A
Time deposit accounts overseas	N/A	48
Merger and acquisition advice overseas	N/A	37

al non-credit services. However, of the 19 per cent of companies which intended to add a bank, nearly a third were doing this because of a rapid increase in the demand for overseas merger and acquisition advice.

Product life cycles in international banking non-credit services tend to be relatively short unless electronically based, and it is important for banks to stay up with the level of service offerings if they intend to compete fully in this sector. In particular the growth of systems based services is seen as a major area for development over the next decade, especially by those large commercial banks seeking to continue to differentiate themselves. Some banks see this area of activity opening up a range of data processing, information management and communication services which provide an opportunity to enter areas of high growth substantially outside the existing bounds of conventional banking.

Electronic banking services will be of great importance in both corporate and retail banking. Once established *via* intelligent terminals, plastic cards or home banking terminals, electronic banking provides a new delivery system which allows the bank to offer an ever-increasing array of services *via* this conduit. In the corporate market therefore cash management products are becoming a necessity for corporate treasurers, offering the opportunity to centralize corporate funds and improve the efficient use of liquid funds, net foreign exchange exposures and the like. New products coming on stream will permit global account interrogation, multicurrency transactions, forward funds forecasting and similar services. In the future, such intelligent terminals can be expected to link to a wide variety of economic and credit data bases and securities data and to permit off-site securities trading. Similarly in retail banking, apart from the widespread use of automated teller machines increasingly in off-bank site locations, electronic systems will be used for direct debit at point of sale, automated bill payments, brokerage dealing, electronic shopping, automatic credit lines and the like. By the mid-1990s electronic banking, both corporate and retail, will become a major delivery system posing a severe threat to conventional branch banking. Further, the strategy for successful electronic banking will open up the financial service market to new competitors from outside the industry and potentially change the entire balance of competitive advantage.

7.5 DEVELOPING BANK PRODUCTS AND SERVICES

The development of new products and services for banks is an important element in marketing. Many services can be developed and introduced with little cost when an establisdhed network of facilities is in place. Similarly, the introduction of many particular services requires the addition of special people and/or systems skills which may well involve a substantial commitment in time and money. As in other industries, it should be remembered that most new services do not prove to be successful and many actually lose money.

Unfortunately the banking industry has traditionally been extremely lax in managing costs, on the grounds that so many bank services share joint facilities and resources that it is impossible to differentiate the costs of specific services. This argument is usually false. As the industry comes under a greater level of competition from both other banks and new industrial and commercial competitors, strict control over service costs will be much more important than in the past.

In addition, it is often argued that banking services are very price-sensitive. This argument too is false. For many services higher product quality can justify higher prices. Careful analysis of service offerings, however, will probably reveal that some services will be highly profitable and relatively price-insensitive while others may be very marginal or even negative in rate of return. As a result, some system for reviewing products or services is required which attempts to optimize the contribution from successful services and terminates inessential loss-makers. One major bank has ranked all its main services using a series of criteria including the following:

1. Operational services which are essential to or closely related to the bank's basic business and which interrelate with other services are desirable. Services unrelated to the bank's business are less desirable.
2. Profitable services are best.
3. Services generating credit and operating risks are less desirable than those that don't.
4. Labour-intensive services are less desirable than automated ones.
5. Float generating services are undesirable.
6. Unique/distinctive services are desirable.

Services within the bank were ranked using such criteria and recognizing that some services might be essential even though they were loss-makers. Each criterion was also weighted to reflect its relative performance and positioned in a two-dimensional matrix such as that in Figure 7.1. The expected future position of the service was also predicted and resource allocation in terms of system/service development made according to its matrix position.

The importance of service quality is becoming increasingly recognized by Japanese banks, who are utilizing techniques developed in manufacturing industry, notably 'quality control circles', to improve this and customer orientation. In one bank 2400 such quality control circles were created, with the groups taking initiative for their own work and looking at how services provided might be better conducted. As a result of these circles, plus other systematic attempts to better understand customer needs, a separate corporate quality control function has been created. The idea of quality control circles is relatively new in Western companies but many manufacturing firms have begun to use the technique with considerable success in Europe and the USA.

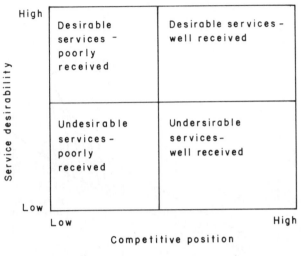

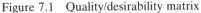

Figure 7.1   Quality/desirability matrix

In designing new financial services, remember:

1. Most new products and services fail as shown in Figure 7.2.
2. The closer you get to actually introducing a new product or service the higher the costs will be, as shown in Figure 7.3.

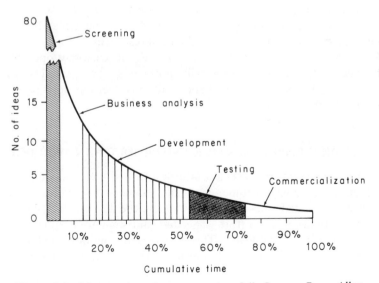

Figure 7.2   Most new products or services fail. *Source: Booz Allen*

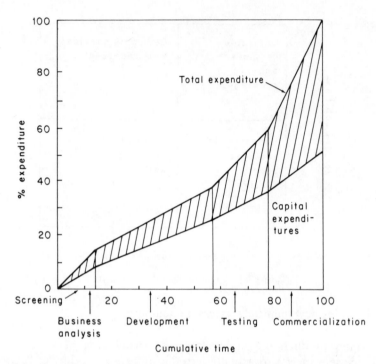

Figure 7.3 Cumulative development expenses rise rapidly approaching commercialization

3. Ruthlessly screen new product and service development with a view to eliminating or amending any doubtful ones before launch and before they have consumed financial and non-financial resources.
4. Phase new service introductions to prevent customer/operations/line management overload. Be especially careful of systems products, which are expensive in cost/time/people and can cause serious loss of customer goodwill if they don't work.

7.6 DEVELOPING SERVICE AND PRODUCT KNOWLEDGE

It is important that the account/branch officers have adequate product knowledge to recognize customer needs and be able to design the correct mix of bank services to satisfy those needs. To achieve the desired level of knowledge substantial attention and effort is needed and regular briefing/motivation/ training is required at all levels. This is especially true in those banks where account officers are seen as relationship managers and represent all bank corporate services to customers.

The service marketing guide is therefore an extremely important vehicle for providing product knowledge. Unfortunately many such marketing guides do not perform the task required of them to assist account officers in their selling duties.

In designing the service marketing guide it is therefore important to ensure that adequate guidelines are established which encourage active business development; such guides should include the following.

Service marketing guidelines

1. *Customer needs.* The customer needs to which the specific service is directed should be clearly identified.
2. *Customer profile.* This should identify the specific segment customer characteristics for whom the service is specifically intended.
3. *Service description.* Outlines the major features of the service which can be used for communication purposes.
4. *Customer service benefits.* Identifies the specific benefits which a customer would expect to gain from using the service.
5. *Bank choice rationale.* Should set out why a customer should choose your bank for this service rather than your competitor.
6. *Problem–solution case.* Should establish in a general way the case 'before' and 'after', showing the typical customer with a problem before adopting the service and the improved result after accepting it.
7. *Instructions for implementation.* Detailed instructions for you to follow when you have gained customer acceptance of the service.
8. *Expected objections and suitable responses.* Should identify the main expected objections from customers and suitable responses which can be adopted by you in your business development presentation.
9. *Follow-up suggestions.* Suggestions for the layout and content of follow-up letters and proposals which describe the service in detail and what the next action steps are for the customer.
10. *Formal acceptance documentation.* Any documentation required to be completed by the branch and/or the customer when the service has been accepted.

7.7 OTHER FACTORS AFFECTING COMMUNICATION

Product range and knowledge alone are not enough to convince and give conviction to customers. They will also be influenced by other characteristics which will color their view of your service range and your ability to deliver the benefits you claim. Most important in this are the image of your bank and of you as an individual.

Factors affecting bank image

— Size
— Nationality
— Awareness
— Perceived image of the market
— Organization structure
— Branch network domestic and international
— Correspondent relationships
— Industry knowhow and specialization
— Geographic knowhow and specialization
— Product and service range
— Management philosophy and policy
— Skills, personality and knowledge of account executive

7.8 CHECKLIST FOR DEVELOPING NEW BANKING AND FINANCIAL SERVICE

In designing banking services, therefore, use the following checklist to ensure you have thought through the key factors for success:

1. What is our purpose in developing this product? Is this consistent with overall unit/division/bank objectives?
2. Which customers is the new service designed for?
3. What precise need is the service designed to meet?
4. How is this need currently met?
5. What share of the market is considered to be open? Attainable?
6. What is the volume and value of the total market? Open market? Attainable market?
7. What will be the reaction of any competition displaced by our entry?
8. What financial resources will be required to develop the service? (Include both on and off balance sheet commitments.)
9. What premises, computer, operations/line lending/branch/staff resources will be required to develop the service?
10. How sensitive is the service to labor cost? Automation?
11. Are these available — if so where and at what cost?
12. What is the lead time for concept development? Service trial? Service introduction?
13. How are the service features expected to compare with those offered by competitors? (Don't forget to also compare expected costs.)
14. How long would it take for competitors to respond?

15. Does the service have distinctive selling features and are these sufficiently attractive to persuade potential customers to adopt our service?
16. Is the service one which would be seen as consistent with our present range and image?
17. Is there any synergy/competition with existing services?
18. What pricing strategy should be adopted for the service? How price-sensitive is the market?
19. How does this compare with that of competitors? Other bank services?
20. Prepare crude expected financial statements for the service. What is the breakeven market share? What is the target ROA market share?
21. Test financial statements for volume/credit risk/country risk sensitivity. Does the service have an acceptable risk profile? If not can this be improved? If not should the service be killed before heavy expenditure is incurred?
22. How would we advise potential customers about the service's existence? Assess advertising spending level/message/media/target audience. Assess personal selling time/training/motivation/opportunity cost.
23. How would we advise those in the bank about the service's existence? Identify training or product literature/targeting/incentive/motivation/time needs.
24. How would we monitor progress? How should we make any necessary amendments to the launch/product/servicing?
25. What back-up services/guarantees/contracts does this service require/imply?
26. What would be the effect of not providing this service on other aspects of the bank's business?

CHAPTER 8

Bank Pricing Strategy

8.1 INTRODUCTION

Price is the key determinant of revenue, while other factors in the marketing mix affect costs. Yet pricing strategy in the banking industry is usually badly developed. Prices tend to be set without reference to overall marketing strategy and without any real understanding of underlying cost structures. This results from the traditional method adopted by banks of bundling their service offerings in a way which disguises the price of individual services in favor of concentrating on overall profitability, usually based on branch economics. Historically the pattern of bank control systems failed to identify the specific costs of providing individual services or servicing individual customers, concentrating rather on profits only at the branch level. Moreover, the principal source of profitability came from the bank intermediary role of achieving an adequate spread on interest rates between the average cost of deposits and the rates charged for loans.

The changing nature of competition in the banking industry is removing the traditional regulatory barriers which encouraged commonality in pricing between similar institutions restricted to operating within specific market areas such as 'commercial banking'. With the breakdown of traditional sector entry barriers as a result of deregulation, new competitors have been able to exploit cost advantages and use pricing tactics to gain market share relative to those institutions still adopting service bundling tactics. In addition, other competitors have been able to maintain price but offer differentiated service quality in order to pick off selected segments on both the retail and wholesale markets.

The transformation from reliance on interest spread differential caused by rising costs of deposits and lower relative interest rates on assets has also led to the growing importance of fee-based income. Here pricing strategies have tended to emphasize one of two directions. In the first of these based on 'skill', product or service differentiation is achieved by the relative uniqueness or creativity of service offerings provided by variable levels of individual skill from different banks. Notably in the corporate market, investment or

142

merchant banks have capitalized on relative skill differentials. However, there has also been a clear trend towards market share gain by the large commercial banks, which have entered this market because of their placing power and ability to commit funds from their own asset bases.

The second direction for pricing strategy has more of a efficiency orientation. With the growing importance of technology-based distribution systems in banking, some form of 'experience' or economy of scale effect has grown in significance. This is especially noticeable in both corporate and retail electronic banking, where costs of providing services have fallen sharply as a result of transaction volume gains. This has tended to emphasize pricing strategies based on market share gain on the part of high technology banks. This in turn has forced those institutions with weak technological positions to either franchise in services from high technology institutions or introduce inefficient competitive services made up of a patchwork of non-integrated systems.

8.2 PRICING OBJECTIVES

In setting price the bank should include this factor as an important ingredient in its overall marketing strategy. For each product market segment it should establish overall strategic objectives and use price as an element in achieving such objectives rather than treat it as an independent factor. Failure to include price in this way will usually lead to inconsistency in the design of segment strategy and contribute significantly to difficulties in achieving desired outcomes. Alternative major objectives that can be established for pricing strategy are as follows.

Current profit maximization

Many banks will wish to set price to maximize current profits. This usually means charging as much as they think the market will bear even when they are unsure of underlying costs and irrespective of long-term strategic consequences. For example, banks have been reluctant to pay reasonable rates of interest on current account balances for up-market consumers until forced to by new-entry competitors such as brokerage companies. As a result many banks have tended to be seen by this customer segment to be offering a poor service and when superior alternatives have become available clients have tended to move to them. This in turn has forced rapid increases in the costs of funds of the banks as they have had to respond by offering money market interest rates to retain their deposit base.

Market share leadership

Although traditionally the impact of market share on the economics of bank services has been limited, the introduction of high technology electronic banking is rapidly changing this. As a result some banks are now actively pricing to maximize market share in order to establish a market leadership position early in service life cycles so as to achieve a higher long-term level of profitability.

Product quality leadership

Some banks may adopt the objective of endeavoring to be the product quality leader in a specific product market segment. This usually means customers will be prepared to pay a somewhat higher price for perceived superior service quality. J. P. Morgan, for example, is seen as providing excellent investment banking services and deep long-term client relationships with the Fortune 500 companies. As a consequence it is able to price its overall service offerings at a level which provides it with superior profitability compared with other US money center banks and despite intense competition for these large accounts.

Capacity maintenance

Many banks faced with substantial overbanking in many countries, especially with the introduction of new delivery systems, and not understanding their underlying cost structures, price services to maximize volume in their branch networks. In many cases this may fail to cover full costs and merely cover variable costs. In some cases, because of inaccuracies in cost analysis, not even marginal costs are fully covered. This is particularly true when banks face new market entrants, especially from non-banks as the result of deregulation. Such organizations, notably retailers, may well have substantially lower cost structures for the delivery of conventional banking services as a result of lower staff, premises and even computing transaction costs.

8.3 ESTIMATING COST STRUCTURE

A critical problem within the banking industry has been the estimation of underlying cost structures. Many bankers have traditionally claimed that it is very difficult to accurately measure service costs due to shared facilities such as branch and central expenses such as computing. As a result they have tended to price on the basis of judgement of the value of the service to customers and without knowledge of underlying costs. Secondly, and again without knowing costs, banks price to meet the levels established by competitors.

An increasing number of banks are now moving towards 'cost visible' pricing where care is taken to establish the underlying costs of individual services by the use of standard costing and operational research techniques. The procedure for establishing such costs is as follows:

1. *Service identification and measurement*

(a) Service identification. Rather than bundling services, these should be carefully separated and individually identified together with a definition of the actitivies making up each one.

(b) Service measurement. Each activity element of the service should be measured to establish a standard time for its performance using established time and motion study methods. Less precise systems involve statistical activity sampling and self time-logging techniques.

2. Cost data base establishment

(a) Staff direct costs. The staff costs per hour for each grade of staff involved in providing a service should be computed. This cost, multiplied by the standard time for each activity element when summed to cover all the activities, provides the direct staff cost of each service.

(b) Other direct costs. All other direct unit costs associated with a service, including telephone, postage, office space rental, computer processing costs, advertising and the like, also need to be identified and added to the direct staff costs.

(c) Overhead costs. Any branch and head office overhead costs not incurred directly in providing a service can also be identified and absorbed to provide a fully absorbed standard cost using an appropriate basis. This area is often one of considerable debate and some banks prefer to use only direct cost standards and contribution margin analysis. In practice both need to be considered.

Once an appropriate basis for overhead cost absorption has been agreed, however, the total standard unit cost of a service can be calculated.

3. Transaction volume analysis

To arrive at the total cost of specific services the unit costs should be multiplied by the appropriate transaction volume. The total service costs calculated can then be compared with actual total costs to test the accuracy of the costing system.

In practice individual accounts make use of a mix of bank services, and given the costs associated with each the relative profitability of each account can be calculated. To undertake such an analysis, however, the bank will usually also require an integrated data base which readily permits the calculation of the cumulative service usage of all the individual accounts of a particular customer and for costs to be compared to revenue. In corporate banking this can be justifiably done on an individual account basis. As a consequence, since the data needs and service usages are usually different to those of retail customers, a growing number of banks are developing two such integrated data bases, one for each class of customer. For retail accounts such an individual customer analysis is usually not an economic proposition for large customer base banks. Here the tendency would be to cluster the account base using cut points in the numbers of transactions, levels of deposit and the like. Such clusters can also be used in conjunction with sociodemographic/lifestyle data for specific customer segments.

The use of standard costing techniques is perhaps best established among Japanese banks. In these institutions the use of standard costing is normal and service standards are checked every six months to ensure continued accuracy. As a result Japanese branch managers are provided with an individual account profitability statement on all their medium and small business accounts on a regular quarterly basis, while profitability analysis for large corporate accounts is available on an online basis. US banks which have introduced standard costing techniques have usually done so by importing specialist cost accounting groups from outside the bank. For example, both J. P. Morgan and Bank of America made use of specialists introduced from the Ford Motor Company. For many European banks, however, the introduction of costing specialists is still in its infancy and heavy use of the major accountancy firms as consultants can be expected over the next few years to introduce relevant techniques and systems.

8.4 STRATEGIC IMPACT AND COST ANALYSIS

The development of standard costs not only provides a basis for establishing the relative profitability of services but more importantly enables the development of strategic options for individual market segments.

8.4.1 The Pareto law Effect

In the banking industry, as in other industrial sectors, the Pareto law effect is normally found. In retail banking it is relatively common that 85 per cent of cost structure on staff, premises, central computer processors and even marketing expenses can be attributed to the bottom 15 per cent of the account base in terms of deposits. This is because the majority of accounts tend to be low on deposits and relatively high on transaction volume.

The traditional bundling of branch operations, where 'free' current account balances were used to cover losses on transaction business, is now giving way to a recognition of the cost of branch operations as interest rate spreads diminish. Banks now increasingly accept that they must recover transaction costs from those customers which incur them, while rewarding with market related interest payments the accounts of low transaction volume and high relative balance customers. As a consequence, many banks are introducing prices related to costs for transaction business, charging differently for machine versus human teller transactions and offering different interest rates for different levels of account balance. A few are going further and actually attempting to shake out unprofitable accounts by discriminatory pricing or deliberate account closures, while introducing superior service at higher prices to preferred accounts.

In the New York retail market Citibank subdivided its retail account base into seven segments. Those with $15,000 or more on deposit were given service by a personal financial advisor in a pleasantly equipped part of the bank. Customers with lower balances were allowed to use the human teller system but were also encouraged to use teller machines. Customers with less than $1000 in deposits were encouraged to bank elsewhere.

This system of segmentation created significant consumer resentment and eventually segregation against low value accounts was technically withdrawn. However, by this time Citibank had largely purified its customer base. This purification even included those corporate accounts for whom Citibank undertook payroll processing and where the bulk of employees instantly withdrew their funds after pay day. As a consequence, because the bank was able to offer a superior service to its better customers by partially eliminating worse customers over a period of five years, it actually doubled its share of the New York retail market. At the same time, the bank reduced its branch network from 260 to 220 branches and its staff from 7000 to 5000, while achieving 70 per cent of cash withdrawals on ATMs, thus substantially reducing its overall cost base.

As a generalization, therefore, you should carefully examine the cost and revenue structures of both customers and services. As shown in Figure 8.1, the probability is that 20 per cent of customers and 20 per cent of services will contribute 80 per cent of revenue. Therefore, rather than continuously adding customers and services indiscriminately and thereby increasing costs but not necessarily profits, look carefully also at rationalizing those accounts and

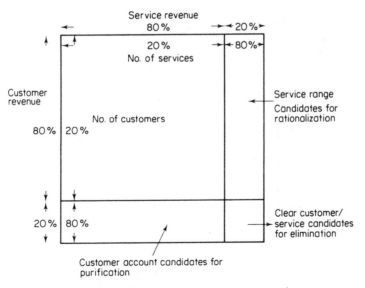

Figure 8.1   Customer service revenue matrix

148

services which may be making losses. The 80 per cent of customers and services which only contribute 20 per cent of revenue are candidates for service rationalization or account purification, and that group of customers and services which intersect in the bottom right-hand corner will almost certainly be running at a loss. Such services or customer accounts should clearly be eliminated unless they can be justified for specific strategic reasons.

8.4.2 The Experience Effect

In many industries a regular decline in costs has been found to occur with cumulated experience. For example, as shown in Figure 8.2 which plots the log of transaction cost in real terms against the log of the cumulative number of transactions, the marginal cost of the one millionth transaction is $1.00. As the bank gains in experience it learns how to do the transaction more efficiently as a result of improvements in systems, staff skills, mechanization, and the like. Thus by the two millionth transaction the marginal cost in real terms has fallen to only 80c and by the four millionth to only 64c. This transaction is therefore said to exhibit an 80 per cent experience effect curve, as every time the cumulative number of transactions doubles there is a 20 per cent decline in costs.

This cost decline does not occur automatically; the assumption is that management is constantly seeking to improve its productivity of operations. Note also that the experience effect applies only to the value added element in

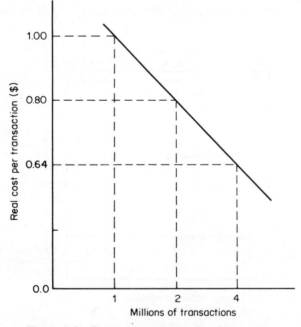

Figure 8.2   Transaction experience effect curve

the provision of a service; that not all competitors need be on the same curve; that 'shared' experience effects are possible as a result of synergy between services using the same facilities such as central processing units; and that the experience effect is volume and not time related.

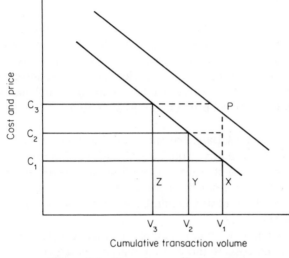

Figure 8.3   Experience effect strategy

Traditionally, experience effects were not especially significant within the banking industry due to regulatory barriers enforcing similarities in cost and price structures. However, deregulation coupled with the introduction of technology-based alternative distribution systems is transforming this pattern. As a result competitive strategy, especially in services affected by electronic technology, favors the adoption of an experience based strategy as illustrated in Figure 8.3. Here bank X has achieved a cumulative transaction volume of V_1, and as a result the bank's marginal cost of further transactions is C_1. To achieve a satisfactory margin for this service the bank offers it to customers at price P, which establishes the market price. Bank Y in contrast has only a cumulative volume of transactions V_2, and assuming it is operating on the same experience curve will have achieved a marginal cost of C_2. However, since the bank must be competitive it can only charge price P for its equivalent service, and hence while still profitable must operate at a lower margin than bank X. Finally, bank Z, which has only achieved a cumulative volume of V_3, will have a cost of C_3. This is above the price P, and hence if bank Z wishes to continue to offer its service it must be prepared to lose money on every transaction.

In high experience effect markets such as electronic banking the achievement of cumulative volume therefore tends to be especially important. As a consequence pricing strategy should endeavor to develop market share rather than achieve short-term profit maximization. Similarly, to increase the effect banks should drive for shared experience by maximizing the range of services using the common delivery system.

In both corporate and retail electronic banking the experience effect is high. As a result, banks like Citibank and Chemical Bank have driven for high market share but by different methods. Citibank has operated independently, building its retail ATM and corporate terminal base as rapidly as possible and utilizing shared experience effects by increasing service range and geographic coverage. Thus its corporate electronic banking is offered on a global basis and by 1984 the bank had some 14,000 terminals on customers' desks offering an increasing array of services. A joint venture with Reuters also enabled Citibank to gain access to the financial information services market and potentially to provide services to Reuters' 39,000 worldwide terminals.

By contrast, Chemical Bank has not sought to take on Citibank head to head but has built cumulative volume and amortized central processor and software development costs over around 8000 worldwide terminals. These terminals, however, have not been placed by Chemical Bank but rather by some 80 bank franchises of its Chemlink corporate cash management systems in the USA and elsewhere.

Competitors unable to build their cumulative experience in electronic banking face similar costs to those of the market leaders but will be unable to price their services to ensure an adequate contribution. Unless such organizations can achieve superior productivity and so move to another, steeper experience curve they should either withdraw from the market, join franchise arrangements with other banks or non-banks, or be prepared to accept that electronic banking will not be the fee income and profit-generating service that many believe it can be.

8.5 PRICING METHOD SELECTION

The selection of a pricing strategy for the bank is a function of three key determinants.

1. *Demand.* The level of demand will be a function of market segment size and service price elasticity. Corporate markets tend to be more price-sensitive than consumer markets. However, different classes of customer will be more or less price-sensitive to specific services and in identifying consumer buying motivations care should be taken to assess these sensitivities.

2. *Competitor prices.* While demand may establish a price ceiling and costs a floor for a service, competitor prices will also help establish pricing range limits. The price and quality of competitor services thus needs to be carefully evaluated as part of competitor analysis. Your bank's services

can thus be evaluated in terms of its overall 'value' compared with competitors to judge what price premium or discount should be charged to best suit your desired strategic position.

3. *Cost structure*. Service cost structure sets the floor for pricing strategy unless for strategic reasons it is considered desirable or necessary to price to make a loss.

Based upon these three criteria a number of pricing options are open to the bank. These alternatives include cost plus pricing, breakeven and profit impact target pricing, value in use pricing, market rate pricing, relationship pricing, penetration pricing and skimming pricing.

8.5.1 Cost Plus Pricing

Cost plus pricing is a simple system of establishing price. Under this method a standard markup is added to the costs of a product or service. Although widely used in the retail trades it is not often employed in banking due to a lack of cost knowledge in many cases. However, because of the similarity with retailing and the expected growth of competition from retailers, especially in retail banking, cost plus pricing may become more important for individual banking services.

As a generalization, however, a pricing method which does not take into account customer price sensitivity and competitive prices does not often lead to the best strategic price. Even in retailing, varied markups for different product groups within the same store have become the norm.

The advantages of cost plus pricing, however, are several. Firstly, if cost structures are well known it simplifies the pricing task. Second, when all similar competitors use this method price competition tends to be reduced. Third, competitors do not have to pay significant attention to demand variations caused by price. Unfortunately, with deregulation the entry of new bank and non-bank competitors with different cost structures may allow the low cost service deliverer to operate a cost plus system (especially in high experience effect services) but force higher cost deliverers to operate a market price related pricing system.

8.5.2 Breakeven and Profit Impact Target Pricing

A second cost oriented pricing method is that of profit impact target pricing. Under this system the bank endeavors to decide on the price which will enable it to achieve a specific level of profitability for a particular service. The method makes use of a breakeven analysis as illustrated in Figure 8.4.

The breakeven chart shows the total cost and total revenue expected at different levels of service transaction volume. First, for each service the level of fixed cost associated with the service is shown. Direct variable costs are added on to these to show a total cost rising with service volume. The total revenue

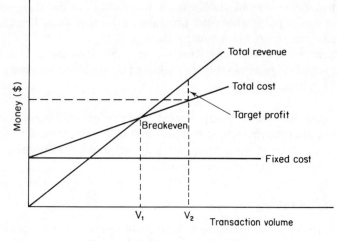

Figure 8.4 Breakeven analysis

curve, starting at zero, usually rises in a linear form with increasing volume. Where the two curves meet is the breakeven volume position V_1, while to meet the desired profit impact target a higher level of volume V_2 is required. In banking fixed costs tend to be relatively high unless staff and premises are treated as variable, and historically these have both tended to be fixed.

In calculating breakeven and profit impact target prices, it is important to check what market share position such a strategy implies. Where it is necessary for the bank to take a high market share to achieve its desired profitability it is important to understand where this share gain will come from. Unless the market segment is high growth, it will usually be necessary for the bank to take share from existing competitors. Since in many cases there is service over capacity, unless the precise competitor has been carefully targeted the likely reaction may be price erosion as established competitors use price in an effort to maintain share. This may substantially change breakeven and profit impact target volumes as revenues decline, and strategies that are very sensitive to competitor price reaction should be examined carefully to test whether the probable end result is worth the effort.

8.5.3 Value in Use Pricing

A number of banks and financial institutions are following industrial companies and basing their price not on cost but on perceived consumer value for a service. This system of pricing requires management to estimate the volume of a service it expects to sell at a specific quality and price. Compared to competitive service offerings it is necessary to assess relative service quality, reliability and the like and to estimate the value that customers would be prepared to pay for these facilities. Adding these to the average competitive base price provides an overall 'value' price for the service. Actual offered prices usually represent a discount from this overall value price, but at the same time such prices are usually above the market average.

An example of such added value service prices is the Merrill Lynch Cash Management Account, which offers up-market consumers not only a checking service but also a Visa card facility, brokerage account, automatic margin loans, money market rate interest on credit balances and investment management facilities. As a result of offering this superior quality of service Merrill Lynch attracted some $70 billion in funds in a few years, much to the chagrin of the banks, who have found it difficult to compete with such an attractive package.

The use of such a pricing strategy, however, infers substantial understanding of your own cost structure as well as that of your competitors. Without such a detailed understanding it is impossible to calculate relative service quality and price between competitors. Moreover, without ongoing market research it is also difficult to check the impact of alternative pricing strategies on customer demand.

8.5.4 Market Rate Pricing

With this system of pricing the bank cedes the initiative to key competitors to set price. Smaller banks 'follow the leader' in pricing services, and while price leaders are usually other banks, non-bank competitors are increasingly influencing service prices as these new entrants may well have operational cost advantage and use price as a conscious weapon to gain market penetration.

For example, the entry by brokerage houses into the market for money market mutual funds had a dramatic efect on the deposit base of US banks, especially those of savings and loan institutions. Offering money market interest rates compared with low fixed rates by the banks, the money funds grew rapidly from the late 1970s. Much of this money was subsequently lent back to the banks in the form of certificates of deposit, significantly raising the banks' cost of funds. When banks were later allowed to compete with the money funds, they were also forced to price their deposit products at competitive rates. In practice, however, most banks were also operating with a substantially higher cost structure due to the high premises and staff costs of their expensive branch delivery system compared with the simple mail or telephone system used by the fund operators.

Nevertheless, market rate pricing remains common with the banking industry due to the lack of cost knowledge. The dangers of this system come from ceding the strategic initiative to competitors and the potential threat of sudden price shifts caused by new entrants or changes in delivery system capability.

8.5.5 Relationship Pricing

While customers are becoming increasingly sophisticated in both corporate and retail markets, leading to service unbundling, there are occasions when services may be provided at a low margin or even at a loss. When it is possible to improve the overall profit from a relationship by cross-selling high margin services, it may be worthwhile to provide relationship-building services in this manner. For example, lead banks may well be prepared to provide difficult sovereign risk facilities at below local market rates to multinational customers provided the overall profitability of the account justifies the decision. Similarly, when corporate customers give the first piece of business to a new bank it tends to be loss-making and is being used as an entry test for the bank. Such business, correctly costed, can be accepted as a marketing cost provided future business from the relationship is expected to yield an adequate level of return.

The concept of relationship pricing is not the same as market rate pricing. It implies the bank clearly knows its cost structure and willingly accepts a low margin or loss in favor of optimizing return on the total relationship. For example, the corporate treasury of ICI asked a number of its lead bankers if they would be prepared to provide the company, at the bank's expense, with one of their best foreign exchange specialists for a year to improve the company's skills at currency arbitraging. All the British clearing banks declined the invitation but the Bank of America willingly accepted in order to improve its overall relationship with the customer. Further, the bank was able to use the publicity associated with its move to gain additional business from other corporations on the premise that if its skills were sought by ICI they must be of an extremely high quality.

8.5.6 Market Penetration Pricing

For new services when high experience effects are present and if the market is price-sensitive, it is best to deliberately price low in order to rapidly build market share and so gain a cost advantage over competitors. Failure to use penetration pricing may well encourage new market entries and provide a price umbrella for the higher cost competitors. Ultimately such a strategy usually leads to a shake-out when a number of competitors exit from the market as a result of a price war due to market overcapacity. The banking industry is perhaps particularly prone to possible overcapacity due to the large number of competing institutions in most countries and an historic tendency to overbanking.

The use of penetration pricing in electronic banking products has proved to be a preemptive weapon and has already led to the forced exit of some competitors while causing other low share competitors to operate at a continuing economic disadvantage. In the New York retail banking market for example, faced with the need for major systems investment to compete effectively, Bankers Trust made the clear decision to withdraw from the market in order to concentrate on wholesale operations.

8.5.7 Skimming Pricing

Skimming price strategy applies when a competitor endeavors to price a service above the normal level of such an activity. For a skimming strategy to be successful there should be a sufficiently large customer segment to justify adopting a skimming price; the costs of operating at lower volume should not be such as to cancel the revenue gain from charging a higher price; the high price should not stimulate the entry of competitors; and the concept of a higher price should add to the image of a superior product.

Within the banking industry, long-term skimming price strategies are not common due to the difficulty of building effective competitive entry barriers. Bankers estimate that in the corporate market most innovative lending products can be rapidly duplicated within a few months at most by new competitors. Further, such innovations cannot be patent protected due to their service nature and the relative ease of creating substitution services.

In the area of electronic banking, it has been possible to generate a distinctive product which has permitted some moderate skimming strategy. The Merrill Lynch Cash Management Account was such a true product innovation, and indeed the systems architecture was sufficiently complex that it did gain limited patent protection. Merrill Lynch, by comparison with subsequent new entry competitors, also priced its product at a somewhat higher rate as a mechanism to indicate exclusivity and superior service image. Copies of this product are now being offered to lower qualifying customers, however, in a variety of forms and some form of cash management account is now becoming a mass market product.

8.6 FACTORS MODIFYING PRICE STRUCTURES

8.6.1 Bank Image

The image of an individual bank or financial institution affects its ability to adopt a specific pricing strategy. For example, a medium-size domestic bank would be unlikely to be able to charge high fees for specialist multinational corporate advice while a retail savings bank would be unlikely to be able to charge a high price for a high net worth private banking advice. It is important therefore that the bank monitors its perceived image to check what services customers believe it can credibly offer and at what level of price.

8.6.2 Impact on Third Parties

The bank must also consider the impact of its pricing policies on others such as shareholders, consumer pressure groups and governments. In the California retail market, for example, consumers are beginning to pressurize banks to provide 'lifeline' banking services for small savers as the banks endeavor to pass on the true cost of operations to customers according to their use of services. Governments, too, are beginning to apply similar pressure on banks which try to purify their customer bases by using price to discourage unprofitable accounts.

8.6.3 Geography

Generally, banks charge different prices for services in different parts of the world dependent upon local money market conditions and regulations. In the large corporate market, however, there is a growing need to price on a global basis. Banks which continue to operate on a localized pricing basis may well find themselves at a strategic disadvantage compared to those which have moved to global account profit planning and hence can allocate price and country risk, for example, against overall account profitability. Such pricing strategy can also be used for global services such as corporate cash management.

8.6.4 Discounts

Discounts in banking usually apply for both volume and value. Large users of services can normally negotiate price with the bank and few banks have clear policies for pricing services to such customers. In part this is due to the failure of banks to adequately understand their costs, but also many banks tend to be volume rather than profit oriented.

Value discounts are offered for example for early payments for debit products, while price premiums may be provided for longer maturities on credit balances. Similarly users of debit cards in point of sale terminals purchasing gasoline in the United States are being offered the same price as cash purchasers. Credit card users by comparison pay a slight premium. In the same way, higher rates of interest are usually offered for term *versus* demand deposits.

In adopting discounts for value or volume, check that the effect is actually consistent with the bank's product market strategy rather than merely responding to either competitor or customer pressure.

8.6.5 Price Discrimination

Banks will often modify their basic pricing to discriminate between customers, product or service form, place and time. With deregulation, price discrimination is becoming of increasing importance in heightening segment entry barriers. Examples of bank service price discrimination include the following.

Customer Discrimination

Different customers pay different prices for the same service or are provided with different service packages at the same price. For example, many banks offer especially favorable terms for students, including promotional items like book allowances. Similarly, a growing number of banks are offering collective discount packages for senior citizen savings account holders.

Product-form Discrimination

Here different versions of the same product or service are priced differently but not proportionately to their respective costs. For example, the relative cost of the American Express green and gold cards is not the threefold price differential which is charged for the use of the latter.

Place Discrimination

Prices differ according to the place in which the service is delivered. For example, many banks now charge a lower price for transactions made on ATMs *versus* the use of counter service tellers.

Time Discrimination

Prices vary according to the time of use of a service. Time discrimination has not yet been used extensively in the banking industry, although such factors as branch opening hours seem likely to become of major importance as deregulation continues.

8.7 SUMMARY

Price is a critical ingredient in the marketing mix for a service or product. Because of regulatory constraints, the use of price as an important element in bank marketing has tended to be neglected. Deregulation, coupled with the introduction of new technology and the arrival of new aggreessive bank and non-bank competitors, is forcing a reappraisal of the use of pricing strategy. At present many banks sacrifice their strategic position by operating market rate pricing because they do not know their own underlying service cost structure.

In the future, banks will be required to undertake regular specialist service cost analysis, build integrated corporate and personal banking data bases and so identify losing services and/or customer segments. Overall marketing strategies will then need to be designed utilizing pricing policy as an essential ingredient to meet the needs of specific customer segments.

8.8 PRICING STRATEGY CHECKLIST

Check your pricing strategy by asking the following questions:

1. What is your present pricing strategy for your service range? Is this policy consistent with overall bank marketing strategy?
2. If you are intent on current profit maximization, will this have a negative impact on your long-term strategic position?
3. If you wish to maximize market share, is this share gain attainable and will it be profitable if you achieve it? Is market share a critical factor in service profitability?
4. If you wish to drive for service quality leadership, do the customer segments for your services perceive your bank as offering superior quality? *Remember* the only measure of service quality is that of the customer, not of the bank.
5. If your objective is capacity maintenance, have you tested your overall strategy for a volume *versus* a profit orientation? Would sacrificing volume for improved profitability be acceptable to top management, who may be size-motivated?
6. How well do you know your services cost structure?
7. Have standard costs been developed for each service? Are these standards regularly updated?
8. Have you checked the contribution effect from particular groups of accounts and services?
9. Have you questioned whether particular services and/or customer groups should be rationalized?
10. Included in such analysis, have you checked whether you are servicing the needs of your best customers as well as you might? Are any new competitors threatening your best customers with superior services priced lower than your own?
11. What services do you offer that exhibit a substantial experience effect? How does your market share compare with leading competitors? Can you compete effectively in the long term in these services?
12. Do you know the effect on demand of different price levels for particular services?
13. Do you really know the pricing strategies of competitors for specific services and/or customer segments?
14. What services could appropriately use cost plus pricing?
15. Do you develop breakeven and profit impact calculations for specific services and alternative pricing strategies? Do you post-audit your successes or failures to find out where you miscalculated?
16. Have you attempted to build up value in use calculations for your services relative to your competitors?
17. If you use market rate pricing, are you satisfied you know whether or not particular services are profitable?

18. Do you make use of penetration pricing for appropriate services?
19. Have you considered skimming price tactics for appropriate services?
20. Are your overall pricing strategies consistent with customer image of your bank?
21. In deciding on pricing strategy, have you contemplated the impact of your decisions on shareholders, external pressure groups and government as well as customer segments?
22. Do you have a global pricing policy for large multinational accounts or global services, or do you operate on a localized geographic branch basis?
23. Do you have a consistent policy on discounting services by volume and/or by value? Is this policy in turn appropriate for your overall product market strategy?
24. Have you adequately segmented your customer base to practise discriminatory pricing where appropriate?

CHAPTER 9

Delivery System Strategy

9.1 INTRODUCTION

In a major review of strategy concluded in 1980, Citibank identified one particular trend which is having a fundamental effect on bank delivery system strategy. The bank concluded that as a result of the development of new, and particularly electronic, delivery systems, by the end of the decade the customer, whether individual or corporate, would determine the time, the place and the method of the banking transaction. If this trend is correct, and the evidence increasingly suggests that it may well be, it potentially transforms the traditional delivery system strategy of banks, which was based on branch banking. In this chapter we will examine branch and alternative delivery systems for financial services, exploring modifications in conventional branch design, branch coverage, electronic banking, telephone banking, home banking, automated teller machine strategy and electronic service delivery systems.

9.2 TYPES OF DELIVERY SYSTEM

Bank delivery systems can be classified according to size, type and the range of services they provide. The most important variants are the full service branch, limited service branch, specialty branch, fully automated branch, thin branch, automated teller machine, financial supermarket and department store financial superstore. In addition, a number of remote electronic delivery systems are growing in importance. These include electronic point of sale (EFTPOS), intelligent terminals, telephone banking and home banking services.

9.2.1 Full Service Branch

The conventional delivery system within the banking industry has been the full service branch. Although graded by size, it is still the case that in many banks virtually all branches, irrespective of size, are said to be able to deliver the full range of products and services offered by the bank to both individual and corporate customers. Since the late 1960s, however, the range of bank services has increased dramatically as deregulation has gradually proceeded and banks have also moved to significantly extend their range of conventional banking service variants. In North America branch architecture has tended to move to an open plan mode as illustrated in Figure 9.1, to encourage the sale of non-transaction services, but in many other countries, notably in Western Europe, branch architecture still tends to stress transaction operations as shown in Figure 9.2.

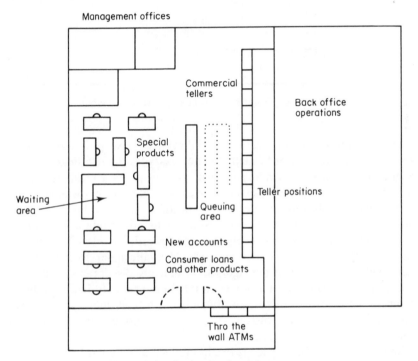

Figure 9.1   Open plan branch structure

The sale of non-transaction financial services in such a branch is made difficult by its reliance on customers taking the initiative to purchase a service by making enquiries at a specific place along the counter system. Such enquiries then require the presence of an executive to handle the request for information. To make the sale it is usually necessary to conduct an interview in a back office area.

This system makes it very difficult for the branch to cross-sell financial services, since it not only relies on preliminary customer initiatives but also on the branch manager or his deputies being available and trained to sell a growing

162

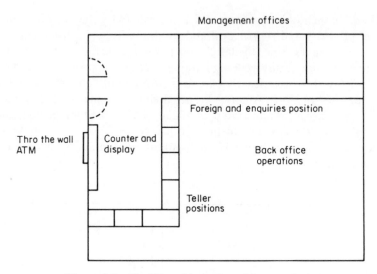

Figure 9.2   Traditional branch architecture layout

profusion of retail and corporate financial services. Except in large financial center branches, there is not usually the necessary level of traffic to justify the presence in the branch of many service specialists. As a result, the limited number of branch management staff have a relatively poor knowledge of many of the services offered in the bank's product manual. Further, branch managers, many of whom were recruited when the sale of financial services via the branch network was neither required nor desired, are often ill-equipped in terms of personality to sell such an array of financial services. Indeed, for several years many branch managers were actively discouraged from selling credit in a seller's market; moreover, their training was to inquire into their customers' credit background, and this has given bank managers a negative image in the eyes of many customers, especially among individual and small business clients.

The rationale for full service is becoming increasingly hard to justify. The traditional reasons for establishing branches were to collect deposits, make local loans and provide a convenience for conducting basic transactions. With the cost of branch-gathered deposits rising rapidly as banks are forced to pay actual or near money market rates of interest, it is possible that wholesale collected funds may actually be cheaper than those taken in the branch. Further, with the advent of alternative transaction methods, especially those that are card or electronic based, there is less need for customers to go to branches to conduct transactions, so reducing the possibilities of any impulse cross-service sales. Finally, again loans can be provided via the alternative delivery systems together with some form of automated credit-scoring system for increasingly higher levels of loan.

As a result, the number of full service branches can be expected to be sharply reduced. Those remaining will be able to justify themselves by the provision of specialist staff handling different segments of retail accounts, and small and medium size corporate accounts while large corporate customers will tend to be handled via a non-branch based account executive system.

Reorganized full service branches will tend to be transformed into limited service operations or specialty branches, or closed. The first stage in full service branch cost reduction is usually to eliminate the existing manager and to downgrade the branch by reducing the level of the future manager. Second, teller positions can potentially be sharply reduced by the use of additional automated teller machines and cash dispensers. Third, the use of online till systems, connected either to central mainframes or to local concentrator branches, can convert many full service branches into satellite operations. This can significantly cut the overall level of personnel needed to manage branch back office operations. Security Pacific, for example, has since 1981 reduced its number of full service branches in the bank's 600 plus branch network in California to around 50, while at the same time the average number of employees per branch has fallen from 14 to eight.

9.2.2 Limited Service Branch

The limited service branch has emerged as an alternative to the full service operation. Offering a strictly limited menu of available services, the 'MacDonalds' style of branch eliminates the need for expensive management and specialist service personnel. In addition such branches, tied to main branches for their data processing, have lower back office costs. Further, reduced personnel needs also allow for smaller space requirements and the average square footage for such branches has fallen from 4000 sq ft to around 2000–2500 sq ft. Even smaller branches are possible when the service range is restricted to basic transaction operations.

9.2.3 Specialty Branch

As deregulation has proceeded, a number of specialty branch operations have begun to emerge as alternatives to full service operations. Such branches tend to focus on either retail or corporate business, but not both. Among the specialist units that have appeared are the following:

Real estate branches. Centered upon mortgage finance, such branches have emerged from conventional savings and loans and building society operations. They have reduced the space devoted to savings and withdrawals and deposit transactions and focused on mortgage customers. In addition to mortgage finance such branches also offer real estate brokerage for both the sale and purchase of property; personal loans, especially for home improvements at higher rates of interest than basic mortgage loans; personal and property insurance; outlets for financial institution backed property development where the bank may be either an equity based developed or construction financier; and potentially, conveyancing and legal services.

High net worth individual branches. Located in appropriate sociodemographic neighborhoods, or inside apartment and condominium complexes, such branches offer a range of banking services for up-market consumers. Based usually on some minimum account balance criterion, such branches offer personal financial counsellor services rather than conventional teller positions and such facilities as previsit telephone withdrawal service, investment counselling and brokerage services, usually in an exclusive, luxurious environment.

Corporate branches. Aimed usually at middle market corporate accounts, such branches do not normally handle retail banking business but offer a range of services specifically directed at medium-sized corporate accounts within a particular geographic area. While the accounts are primarily serviced by an account officer structure centered on the branch, the outlet itself will usually offer specific services such as online foreign exchange, letters of credit, asset based finance specialization, corporate cash management services and the like, rather than expecting the account officers to be specialists in all those service offerings.

Representative offices. A low-cost variant of a full corporate branch, technically representative offices cannot write business but merely act as an introductory system for full service outlets. Such offices are cheap to operate, and are often a prelude to expansion to full branch status.

Loan production offices. These are non-deposit taking offices which can write asset business and have been used especially in the United States by corporate oriented commercial banks to cross state boundaries.

9.2.4 Fully Automated Branches

In a drive to improve productivity and cut costs still further, the fully automated bank branch has begun to appear in a number of countries. Perhaps most advanced in Japan, such units provide a range of machines within the area of the branch which enable the customer to undertake most basic bank transactions. Such a branch is illustrated in Figure 9.3.

In this branch, which does not use especially advanced technology, cash deposits and withdrawals, balance enquiries and interaccount transactions can be conducted by the customer without bank employee intervention. Two employees are present in the branch to assist customers in using the machines

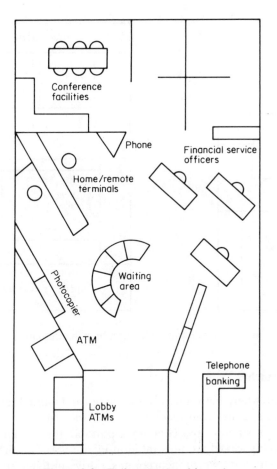

Figure 9.3   Fully automated branch

and also to provide advice on non-automated services such as investment management and the like. Such branches, while operating with few or no staff, have also substantially reduced space requirements of 800–1500 sq ft since there are no on-site back office operations. The use of fully automated branches appeals to only a limited segment of the population, however. These individuals are usually younger than 35 and relatively well educated. The most advanced automated branches in Western Europe are operated by the Verbrauche Bank in West Germany. This bank, which only operates automated branches, was acquired early in 1984 by the largest German mail order retail company, Schickendanz, which intends to use the bank's technology to link its mail order and retail store operations in order to provide a comprehensive automated consumer shopping and financial services range of activities.

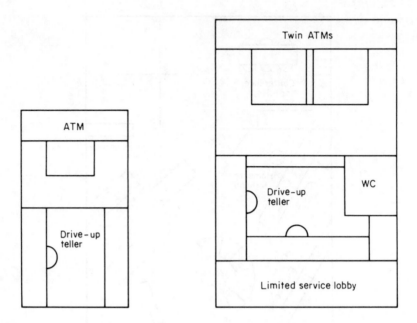

Figure 9.4   Prefabricated thin branch alternatives

9.2.5 Thin Branches

Positioned somewhere between fully automated and limited service branches, these branches operate from readily available sites such as supermarket car parks and petrol stations and come in a portable form from the back of a truck. Two such variants are illustrated in Figure 9.4. The first of these is a prefabricated structure which incorporates a drive-in teller at one end and a 24 hr automated teller unit at the other. Such a unit can be delivered to convenient sites as available and can be subsequently moved to other sites if required. The second structure is a two-teller version which enables a limited range of desk services to be provided such as account opening and the like. The use of such prefabricated units enables banks to substantially increase their number of distribution points at a fraction of the cost of full branch openings.

Thin branches offer a similar low-cost alternative to permanently sited thin branches. Such units are especially useful for providing service to industrial customers for whom the bank may undertake a payroll service. Because conventional branch opening hours are highly inconvenient for many industrial workers, banks have found it difficult in some countries to convert cash-based wage payment systems into magnetic tape based bank credit accounts. The use of mobile branches and remote on site ATMs to provide cheque or card based cashing facilities is a mechanism for giving some form of service to customers who would otherwise find the use of banks unacceptably inconvenient.

9.2.6 Automated Teller Machines

The installation of automated teller machines has expanded rapidly during the 1980s. By the end of 1984 the number of ATMs installed in the United States was estimated at 45,000, up from 13,800 in 1979. In Western Europe at the end of 1982 the number of machines installed was estimated at over 11,000, similarly up from 3850 in 1980. In Europe around half these machines were installed in France and the UK, while installations in Western Germany were notably lower. In Japan, however, compared with their relatively small number of branches, the major city banks had the highest number of ATMs installed per branch than any other banks in the world. A list of major banks, their branch coverage and ATM installations is shown in Table 9.1.

Table 9.1
Bank ATM and Branch Network Coverage 1984

Bank	No of ATMs	No of domestic offices	ATMs/branch
Credit Agricole	2400	10,800	0.22
Lloyds Bank	1556	2467	0.63
National Westminster	1349	3637	0.37
Dai Ichi Kangyo	1346	345	3.9
Mitsubishi Bank	1082	227	4.7
Fuji Bank	1052	257	4.09
Sumitomo Bank	1030	232	4.44
Taiyo Kobe Bank	976	335	2.91
Sanwa Bank	966	252	3.83
Bank America Corp.	409	1243	0.73
Mibui Bank	843	194	4.35
Citicorp	547	980	0.56

Source: Retail Banking International.

The use of automated teller machines has also expanded rapidly as consumers have increasingly come to accept them. In fact, market research studies in a number of countries have shown that in many cases bank customers actually prefer to conduct their transactions on ATMs rather than using human tellers. As machines have gained in acceptance and the number of installations has risen, the cost of transactions by machine has gradually fallen.

In the USA it is estimated that the cost of conducting a transaction on the ATM versus using a human teller was approximately the same in 1982. Since that time machine transactions have been lower in cost as machine prices have fallen and transaction volume has risen, while transactions with human tellers have increased in cost as labor rates have risen. In other countries similar trends can be detected, and by the end of 1985 it is estimated that in most developed countries ATM transaction costs will be lower than those involving human tellers.

Initially the great majority of ATMs were installed in the lobbies or through the walls of existing banks and savings and loan institutions. For suburban banks ATMs were also provided on bank sites for drive-in utilization. Increasingly, however, new ATM installations are occurring in off-site locations with high levels of traffic flow such as airports, railway stations, shopping centers and especially supermarkets and convenience stores. In the USA a substantial number of supermarket and convenience store retailers are installing on their own behalf, or in conjunction with banks or non-bank ATM operators, extensive machine networks. Moreover, unlike many banks, retailer installed ATMs strive for universality to maximize the number of card holders who can access machines on their premises. In this way the retailers anticipate being able to provide a convenience attraction which will help to lure retail custom for their traditional services while at the same time generating significant revenue from effectively renting their floor space to ATM operators in return for a percentage of individual transaction charges. The same trend of growing retail involvement is also occurring in Western Europe, where a number of major retailers in the UK, France, Belgium and West Germany are experimenting with or have announced plans to install ATMs in their stores.

The desire by retailers for universality for all card holders to be able to access machines on their premises has been shared by a number of banks. As a result in the United States there has been a rapid growth in the number of ATMs linked by some form of shared network. Some of these work in localized geographic areas while others cover much of the country. In France the largest overall shared network links the electronic point of sale and ATM networks of all the leading banks. In Germany moves are in train to create a Europewide electronic card access system based on the Eurocard. Finally, the two leading credit card companies Visa and Mastercard are endeavoring to create global ATM access systems for the cardholders of member banks.

ATMs have become an important delivery system for cash withdrawal, deposits, balance reporting and interaccount transfers in retail banking. The number of ATMs installed is still increasing at around 30 per cent per annum worldwide and their growing numbers pose a substantial threat to traditional transaction based branches. This is especially true for new ATM installations, which will tend increasingly to be off bank sites and relatively universal in the cards that will be able to access them. For banks the installation of further ATMs must be carefully considered as a component in overall delivery system strategy, and where such installations are undertaken consideration should at the same time also be given to the size and shape of the existing branch network.

9.2.7 The Financial Supermarket

As a result of deregulation it has become possible either directly or indirectly to operate a supermarket for financial services within the retail market. Such a concept brings together normal banking services and services traditionally handled by other specialist institutions with barriers to entry created largely by official regulations. Such services usually include stocks and shares brokerage, and as part of their product market strategies many banks have moved rapidly to acquire outright or to achieve strategic stakes in, leading brokerage companies around the world. They also include insurance which is still not a permitted service offering for banks either as brokers or as underwriters in some leading countries, notably the United States. This restriction where it persists can still be avoided, however, by franchising branch space to established insurance brokers or direct sales underwriters. Finally, the financial supermarket may well offer real estate finance and brokerage services, and already Lloyds Bank has become the largest real estate broker in the UK while Sears Roebuck and Merrill Lynch have both built national retail real estate brokerage chains in the USA.

By offering all these financial services under the same roof, banks hope to spread branch overhead expense costs while at the same time increasing the appeal of the branch to users of each of the specialist services offered. As a result it is hoped branch space utilization will improve. In addition such branches may be laid out so as to stimulate the use of extra services by placing the transaction component of the bank towards the back. Under such a system it is necessary for transaction users to pass open plan desks or areas offering the additional services. Conventional financial services may not, however, be sufficiently popular to generate substantial branch traffic volume of themselves, and as a consequence some institutions have been exploring the use of related services which have better capability of generating floor traffic. Such other traffic generator services which have been considered and in some cases offered include travel services and consumer credit finance facilities. Whether this multiservice strategy offered by banks and other financial institutions will succeed is, however, still unclear.

9.2.8 The Department Store Financial Supermarket

Deregulation has brought the invasion of the financial services industry by major retailers. A number of these are beginning to offer a range of financial services to their established customer bases. Moreover, for such institutions the entry barrier into financial services is relatively low. They already possess large established client bases. For example, while the largest bank card client base in the USA is Citibank's, with around 11 million card holders, Sears Roebuck's charge card base is over three times this number. Further, they have traditionally been strong in retail revolving credit finance, usually written on their own book.

After purchasing the brokerage firm, Dean Witter Reynolds and real estate brokerage operator Coldwell Bank, Sears Roebuck began experimentally to open financial service centers in their existing retail stores in 1983. In the state of California, Sears also offered banking services after purchasing a savings and loan bank. Following successful experiments by the end of 1984, Sears planned to have 300 in-store financial centers open offering insurance, real estate and investment brokerage services. By 1986, the number of such outlets was expected to rise to 600 nationwide.

In offering financial services in-store, Sears Roebuck has a number of significant advantages. Firstly, the store group's image for quality and reliability inspires confidence, especially among middle American consumers. Second, Sears automatically has the store traffic generated by its department store merchandise range, unlike a competitor bank which has no such traffic. Third, Sears has an established customer base using its in-house credit card facility, and also its catalog sales purchasers who can provide automatic target audiences for advertising messages about Sears' financial service offerings. Fourth, in its advertising Sears stresses the relative differences in its store opening hours compared with those of the banks. Sears' financial centers are open 10 am till 9 pm Monday to Friday, 10 am till 5 pm on Saturdays and 12 am till 4 pm on Sundays. Finally, relative staff and premises costs for the retailer have been estimated at around 60 per cent of those of a commercial bank due to lower relative rental costs and a combination of lower actual costs and longer opening hours for employees.

Sears' pattern of entry into financial services has been eagerly monitored by many other lending retailers who believe they have a similar retail image to Sears. As a result leading department stores, mail order operators and up-market supermarket groups are actively contemplating or have decided to enter the financial services industry in a significant way. Around the world, therefore, the financial services supermarket concept is being developed as an active component of strategy by leading retailers.

9.2.9 Electronic Point of Sale

Electronic funds transfer at the point of sale (EFTPOS) offers a cashless method of payment to the consumer at the point of purchase. The leading exponents of electronic point of sale are not bankers but actually the gasoline retail companies. These organizations not only wish to provide consumer convenience but also to reduce their float tied up in credit operations. Further, they see electronic point of sale as a prerequisite to the introduction of unmanned gasoline stations. EFTPOS will, however, also be important in all areas of retail transactions, although at present there remain considerable differences between retailers and bankers about who manages the EFTPOS network and also who pays for hardware and software development.

In many countries EFTPOS schemes proposed by banks have run into difficulty as the banks have endeavored to charge more than retailers have been prepared to accept. While EFTPOS will doubtless become an important payment mechanism it is not expected to wholly replace cheques, although successful EFTPOS systems are likely to reduce cash payments and in particular stimulate the use of debit rather than credit cards. As with ATMs, EFTPOS also reduces the need for consumers to visit the branch network.

9.2.10 Intelligent Terminals

In the corporate market, developments in electronic banking have led to the introduction of intelligent terminals. With these, and backed up with their own central processing units, corporate treasurers can interact with the bank's own mainframe computers to undertake cash management, transactions, letters of credit and the like, receiving timely transaction data and other economic and financial information services.

The introduction of intelligent terminal delivery systems has advanced most rapidly in the United States, where it is quickly becoming the norm in the large and increasingly the medium corporate market. In Western Europe such systems are being introduced but, apart from large multinational corporations, penetration is still low. In Japan, 'firm' banking was only permitted by the regulatory authorities in 1983 but is gaining rapid acceptance. The strong experience effect in this service means that competing banks should drive for early market share gain. As a result, aggressive competitors such as Citibank and Chemical Bank have been striving to quickly build up their installed terminal base during the rapid growth phase of this delivery system.

9.2.11 Home Banking

The corollary of intelligent terminals in retail banking has been the introduction of home banking. Utilizing a microcomputer or other form of terminal and linked by telephone or videotex, home banking experiments are taking place in most developed economies. In the United States some such systems have already been launched commercially but the number of subscribers are currently few, although with the rapid expansion of home-based microcomputers the potential user base is expanding rapidly.

Normally home banking is likely to be just one of a range of services provided as part of a home information system which also offers shopping, news, entertainment and information data. The home banking service itself will usually permit account interrogation, interaccount transactions, bill payments, loan generation and electronic mail. In addition some systems are adding brokerage, insurance and mortgage banking facilities. By the end of the decade home banking is expected to become a significant alternative delivery system to conventional branch systems but is presently still of limited importance.

9.2.12 Card-Based Systems

Card-based delivery systems have rapidly expanded the array of services they are capable of delivering via a variety of distribution outlets including banks, stores, airports, ATMs and the like. The future potential of cards still seems considerable as 'smart' cards with memory capability provide new opportunities for service expansion. Already Citibank's Focus Account Card based service is stated to be able to deliver some 30 products or services to card holders, with services being accessed in a variety of bank and non-bank outlets.

9.2.13 Telemarketing and Distance Delivery Systems

The larger 'branch' of Manufacturers Hanover with $250m of deposits has no customers visit it. The 'branch' customers reside throughout the USA and their deposits have been solicited by long line telemarketing and direct mail. There has been a substantial growth in both credit and deposit service sold via direct mail, telemarketing and direct response newspaper advertising. These systems are much cheaper than full branch operations and are especially useful to banks which do not have high involvment in nationwide bricks and mortar.

9.3 TRENDS IN DELIVERY SYSTEM STRATEGY

As a result of deregulation and increased market segmentation, there has been a sharp increase in bank service distribution outlets. However, while the number of traditional branches grew slightly or was stable in most countries during the 1970s, the 1980s have seen a sharp decline trend in their numbers. Meanwhile the numbers of machine and electronic delivery system outlets have grown dramatically. Overall, in both corporate and retail banking there has been a growing choice of delivery system, much greater time flexibility and a variety of methods of undertaking financial transactions. Moreover, distribution outlets have tended to become increasingly specialized and directed towards specific groups of customers. The most obvious of these trends has been the growing move to provide different outlets for retail and corporate accounts as part of the strategy of dividing individual and institutional banking.

The squeeze on interest margins, pressures for service unbundling and the need to provide improved quality to selected customer groups has forced banks to both add expensive new delivery systems and reexamine the cost of maintaining traditional distribution methods. While heavy investment has therefore been taking place in electronic delivery systems, disinvestment, closures and cost rationalization are now occurring in traditional branch systems.

For branch-based banks the critical costs in operations have always been staff and premises. While spread differentials remained high, banks could, and did, afford to pay above average in salaries and fringe benefits. Today banks can no longer afford such luxuries as loan loss rates rise, spreads narrow and return on equity falls to levels which make the raising of new equity funds difficult. As a result, with the introduction of more machine and remote distribution outlets banks are being forced to cut the costs of traditional branch offices. This is occurring in a variety of ways, notably:

Branch closures. In the United States many banks have announced branch closure plans. For example, the Bank of America in California is closing around a third of its overall network while increasing its number of ATM installations and introducing home banking. Branch closures are also occurring among international branch networks which were expanded rapidly during the 1970s. Many of these branches, operating largely in the corporate market in world financial centers, have consistently been unprofitable. In Japan, for example, the majority of most international bank branches were operating only marginally profitably in 1983. For many banks the initial desire to service large-scale multinationals via a global branch network has given way to a more focused strategy on a more limited geographic, customer or service base, leading to a rationalization of unnecessary, expensive international branches.

More limited service branches. To cut costs, a growing number of banks are relying more on limited service branches or thin branches. For example, in the United Kingdom Barclays has announced plans to cut its 3000 plus network of full service branches by half. After some 100 closures, half the remaining branches are being converted either to limited service satellite branches or to agency or support branches of the machine and teller variety.

Increased specialist branches. Many banks are trying to convert existing branches into specialist units where the level of customer support will justify it. In particular, medium corporate branches are emerging as important in major cities, while real estate and high net worth individual branches appear to be of growing importance in retail banking.

Automated branch experimentation. Many banks are experimenting with a variety of automated branch formats. Operating a limited number of services notably for retail customers, existing automated branches have proved only partially successful, appealing to a special technologically oriented customer segment. At present, therefore, automated branches are not a significant element in delivery system strategy and it is still unclear as to how well the concept will be accepted.

Electronic and machine banking. Virtually all banks are incorporating greater elements of electronic banking in their delivery system strategies. ATM utilization is growing, although many banks do not enjoy good utilization rates for machines as a result of poor marketing, bad siting or both. For successful ATM introduction great care must be taken to ensure easy use, good site selection and adequate marketing to build the customer card base. For smaller banks linkages to joint networks are also important to reduce overhead and systems development costs.

Electronic terminal banking for both corporate and retail sectors is also of growing importance. Corporate intelligent terminal banking will rapidly become common, although retail home banking is unlikely to form a major element in customer services for some years. Again for smaller banks the cost of electronic service development are potentially prohibitive and therefore such institutions are likely to rely more on franchised or shared systems.

9.4 THE OUTLET LOCATION DECISION

In deciding upon its delivery system strategy, the established branch bank today is forced in most cases into a mixed delivery system strategy. For new entrants the choice of delivery system strategy may be more open; dependent upon the service range and customer base covered by overall product market strategy. Thus organizations without established branch networks may seek to reach a segment of a wider market by adopting only electronic, telephone or direct mail service delivery systems, using price to offset the lower service quality of a non-physical presence. Some form of physical presence is usually necessary, however, for anything other than a limited segment service range strategy. A critical ingredient in such a strategy is the outlet location decision. In this decision process the following steps need to be considered:

1. Evaluate the territory in terms of the customer characteristics, corporate or retail, and competitor bank strategies.
2. Decide what type of delivery system outlet is most appropriate for the geographic area.
3. Select the type of location that is most appropriate for an isolated unit, unplanned business direct or planned shopping center complex.
4. Analyse and decide between alternative sites of the appropriate location type.

The area over which a banking outlet operates can be divided into three parts as shown in Figure 9.5, namely primary, secondary and fringe. The

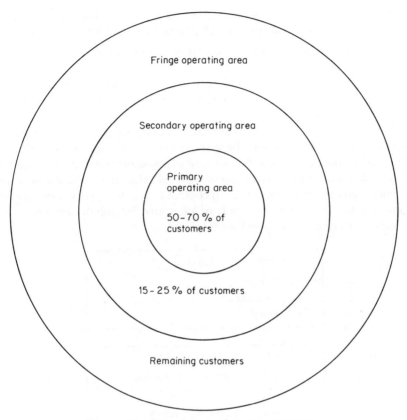

Figure 9.5   Branch operating area segments

primary operating area embraces 50–75 per cent of branch customers and is the area closest to the branch with a minimum of overlap with other branches.

The secondary operating area contains a further 15–25 per cent of customers. Customers from this area are more widely dispersed and there may be different overlaps with different branches or outlets. The circular pattern shown in Figure 9.5 need not be characteristic and the actual operating area will be determined by a number of other factors such as number and type of branch outlet, location and density of competition, actual travel time and mode of travel, and location surroundings. For example, bank branches are relatively low traffic generators, even parasites, whereas certain types of retail stores are high generators and adjacent bank branches may well gain from spin-off traffic.

The size and shape of the branch operating area can be determined relatively accurately from a study of branch records. Such investigations can be improved by additional trend analysis and specific surveys to measure actual and potential changes in operating area traffic volume. The value of specific areas

176

for individual service volumes can also be calculated based on patterns such as Reilly's law[1] or refinements proposed by Huff[2] and Gautschi[3] as follows:

Expected annual service use = number of customers by segment in the area
$\times$
percentage of customers in area using your outlet
$\times$
annual expected service use per customer.

Thus the nature of the customer base and the type of services used by different sociodemographic groups can be included to assess branch or outlet potential. For this analysis it is possible to assess the total value of a particular area and, coupling these data with the degree of competitive activity, some estimates can be made as to the economic viability of alternative branch or outlet strategies for particular areas as shown in Figure 9.6.

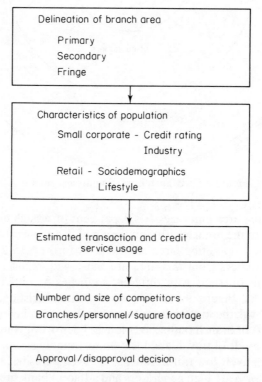

Figure 9.6

[1] William J. Reilly, Method for the Study of Retail Relationships, Research Monograph No. 4 (Austin University of Texas Press, 1929), University of Texas Bulletin No. 2944.
[2] David L. Huff and Larry Blue, *A Programmed Solution for Estimating Retail Sales Potential* (Lawrence: University of Kansas), 1966.
[3] David A. Gautschi, Specification of patronage models for retail choice,

9.5 SUMMARY

The choice of delivery system for the individual bank has become a critical strategic issue. In evaluating delivery system strategy the bank must first evaluate its overall product market strategy and determine the most appropriate geographic coverage and outlet type to meet the service needs of its served market customer base. Moreover, care must also be taken to evaluate the future trends in these served market customer needs and in various delivery system cost structures. Evaluating specific outlet sites should be done in a rational manner, by evaluating various service modes and estimating the economics of such alternatives. In particular, care must be taken not to treat the existing branch network as an inflexible system which must be preserved at all costs. Such an attitude will lead to more agile competitors potentially gaining and using important cost advantages to achieve a competitive edge.

9.6 EVALUATING DELIVERY SYSTEM STRATEGY

Delivery system strategy is becoming a critical area for bank strategic decision-making as a result of new technology and deregulation offering a growing choice of channel. Evaluate your present and proposed strategy using the following checklist.

1. What is the make-up of your existing service delivery system?
2. How appropriate is the system for reaching the customer segments you have identified in your served market?
3. What delivery systems are being used by competitors and with what degree of success?
4. How saturated is your served market with each type of delivery system?
5. What is the trend for each type of delivery system?
6. How do you estimate the costs of each alternative system? How do your costs compare with system averages and those of critical competitors?
7. Have you evaluated your overall delivery system strategy to ensure it is consistent with technological, customer and competitive trends?
8. Is any part of your delivery system a sacred cow?
9. Where necessary, have your systems been rationalized?
10. Where significant experience effects operate, can you afford to play the game? If not, what franchise/acquisition or technology buy-ins are available?
11. Is your research and development of delivery system development adequate in terms of money, people, software and hardware?
12. Do you adequately evaluate site alternatives for various delivery system options?
13. Do you consistently monitor demographic changes in your branch operating areas to ensure that your delivery system strategy is current?
14. Have you developed adequate decision support systems to undertake quantified site evaluation?

CHAPTER 10

Communications Strategy

10.1 INTRODUCTION

Communications strategy has become an important ingredient in bank marketing strategy. Since the early 1970s when banks paid little attention to communications they have been forced to spend heavily on advertising, publicity and personal selling, the relative mix depending upon the specific market segment to which they have attempted to appeal. The four major elements in communications strategy are as follows:

1. Advertising. This is a non-personal vehicle for presenting and promoting services and image for a bank or financial institution. A dramatic growth has occurred in the level of bank spending for services directed both to individuals and to corporations. Banks have also engaged in image advertising.
2. Public relations. This form of non-personal communication attempts to present the bank in a favorable light in news stories and other media coverage which is not specifically paid for directly. Such activities include news releases, officers' speeches, sponsorship of external events and the like. Banks have made substantial use of sponsorship of sporting, cultural and charity events for image public relations.
3. Promotion. Important for retail banking, this involves the use of short-term incentives to encourage the purchase of specific services. In the late 1970s, for example, the New York 'toaster wars' involved giving away consumer appliances of various values in return for different levels of deposits.
4. Personal selling. Because of its expense, personal selling tends to be used in the banking industry only to those segments which can justify the cost. Account and relationship managers are becoming the norm in middle and large corporate banking, but in individual banking personal selling tends to be confined to high net worth individuals.

There are many variants of each of the four main communication elements as shown in Figure 10.1. One problem for banks which makes the communication

178

Advertising	Public relations	Promotions	Personal selling
Print ads	Press kits	Giveaways	Branch managers
TV & radio ads	Speeches	Fairs & trade shows	Account officers
Cinema ads	Seminars	Exhibits	Relationship managers
Mailings	Annual reports	Demonstrations	Personal inv. managers
Directories	Sponsorship	Special discounts	Telemarketing
In branch leaflets		Free banking	Seminar selling
Display signs		Special investments	
Promotional magazines			
Audiovisual materials			
Brochures & bulletins			

Figure 10.1   Communications system variants

task more difficult is that for most service offerings there is no physical product that consumers can see. This makes it especially important to describe the service clearly and to identify the benefits that can be expected to accrue from its use and that satisfy customer needs.

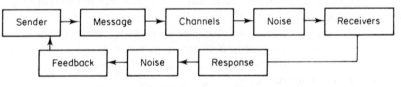

Figure 10.2   The communication process

A message is sent from the sender to the desired audience via a communication channel. (Figure 10.2) This in turn results in feedback from the audience which may or may not be the action desired by the sender. When an unwelcome result occurs, this is due to system noise, which results in the wrong message being received. This communication failure occurs for a variety of reasons, including:

1. Selective attention—Occurs when the audience only listens to part of the message because of heavy exposure to many other and often conflicting messages from other senders.
2. Selective distortion—Occurs when the audience twists the message it hears to mean something else.
3. Selective recall—Occurs when the audience only recalls a small part of the message.

4. Feedback distortion—The response by the audience may be similarly misinterpreted by the sending bank as a result of noise in the feedback mechanism. The role of communications strategy is therefore to cut through the noise to provide a clear message to the receiver which results in actions desired by the sender.

10.2 DEVELOPING COMMUNICATIONS STRATEGY

The process of developing communications strategy is illustrated in Figure 10.3. Communications strategy forms an essential component in the design of overall marketing strategy. As such, an appropriately developed strategy will identify *what* message to communicate, to *whom, where, when, how often, by what means* and at *what cost* to achieve expected objectives. The strategy, once implemented, should be carefully monitored to check if it is achieving its objectives, and if not either the marketing strategy, objectives or communications plan will need to be modified.

10.3 PERSONAL SELLING

Personal selling has traditionally been the principal communication channel in the banking industry, although until recently the concept of selling financial services was very poorly developed. Nevertheless the branch delivery system and the branch manager in particular were seen as the key to client interface. In corporate banking personal selling is still the preferred means of communication and in the large and medium corporate market specialist account managers have tended to supersede traditional branch managers as the main mechanism for the bank to sell its services. The role of this form of personal selling is discussed in detail in Chapter 6.

In the small corporate market the role of the branch manager remains critical but in this sector non-personal selling is also important, especially in lead generation. The branch manager operates on a geographic territorial basis, covering the area around his branch and being responsible for selling an exceptionally wide product range for a full service branch. In addition, the branch manager and his staff are also an important interface for the sale of personal financial service products. In this area, however, branches have become of significantly less importance due to greater use of direct mail, the press, tie-in deals with providers of other products and services and the development of electronic delivery systems. The rising cost of personal selling also threatens to continue to restrict the level of service which can justify the provision of person-to-person communication. Moreover, the emergence of alternative delivery systems means that customers, both personal and corporate, have less and less need to visit branches, where banks have traditionally concentrated their personal selling efforts.

Unfortunately most branch bank managers were also recruited not as

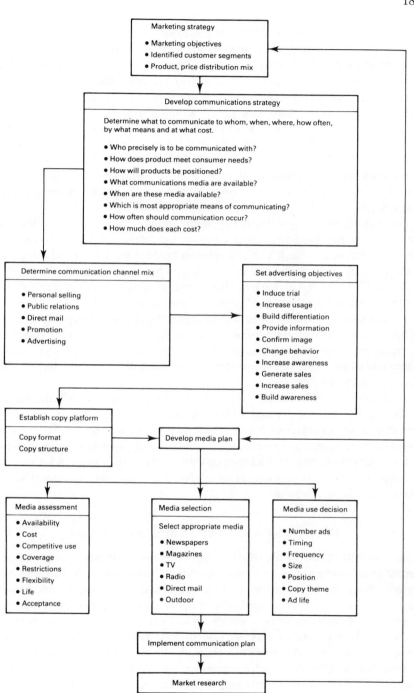

Figure 10.3 Developing communications strategy

salesmen but rather as administrators, and banks face a major reeducation or personnel replacement task to convert their existing branch outlets into attractive centers for the sale of financial services. The role of personal selling as a commuinication channel may therefore change significantly in banking. Customer, rather than geographic, specialization is likely to grow in importance for larger corporate markets, and also the provision of personal finance counsellors for the high net worth individual segment in retail banking. The provision of services to other personal clients and for small business will tend to rely less on personal selling and more on the use of off-site semi-automated or automatic services such as retail revolving credit loans, credit-scored in-store consumer finance, and off-site salespersons in centers such as car showrooms, retail stores and the like.

Innovative, more cost-effective personal selling techniques such as telemarketing and seminar selling for both corporate and personal finance services will also be introduced. Such vehicles tend to be best used for product-specific concepts such as Bank of America's foreign exchange management seminars or Chemical Bank's IRA seminars. These seminar techniques do not rely wholly on personal selling but are usually enhanced by the use of audiovisual techniques such as videos and audio cassettes which may incorporate popular actors; these improve presentation and allow for the development of consistent professional standards. Such standardized presentations are then supported by personal selling professionals in after-presentation discussions to follow up or complete service sales.

In developing the role of personal selling in the bank's overall communications strategy, the requirements for each key client group should be assessed and objectives for different forms of personal selling developed. Strategies to provide the necessary resources including retraining, sales skills education and sales support materials should then be established. The impact of introducing these policies then needs monitoring against the objectives to ensure that they achieve the desired results.

10.4 PROMOTION AND PUBLIC RELATIONS

Sales promotion and public relations have increased sharply in importance in recent years, especially in consumer markets. Promotion tools include a wide variety designed to stimulate or enhance market response which may be generated by other components of communications and marketing strategy. Such tools include samples, contests, prices-off, premiums and demonstrations. Trade promotions may also be offered when bank services such as consumer finance are provided through third parties like retailers or automobile distributors. Such promotions include special volume discounts, free goods, cooperative advertising, dealer sales contests and dealer salesmen incentives. Within banks themselves incentives are being increasingly offered for superior performance. Many banks now offer bonuses for meeting sales objectives or other incentives such as contests, free goods and holidays. Promotion techniques tend to be faster in operation than advertising but the response to them is also usually shorter in duration and not especially likely to affect basic customer loyalty. As such, promotions attract deal-oriented consumers who are likely to switch banks rather than new long-term accounts. By contrast, advertising is more likely to capture new 'permanent' accounts. Promotion can be especially helpful, however, in increasing awareness and image of new services by existing customers and used in this way can form a valuable element in communications strategy.

Public relations is more of a background activity and is designed to enhance the bank's position with specifically targeted audiences. Sponsorship has thus become an important activity in developing bank image. Such sponsorship can be directed to specific target customer segments such as accountants, farmers, culture lovers and sports players. The key objective of publicity is to obtain editorial coverage, as distinct from paid space, in media seen by the bank's desired customer base. It may be used to promote services, places, ideas, people, activities and organizational image.

The results of publicity can, however, be especially important and close attention to public relations can lead to substantial strategic advantage. This is especially important for institutions with low communications budgets since publicity is generally much cheaper than direct mail and media advertising.

10.4.1 Setting Sales Promotion Objectives

It is important to establish what the objectives are for a sales promotion before it is introduced and to anticipate the likely competitive response. Such objectives might be to encourage more usage, to develop trials amongst non-users and to attract new accounts. For trade accounts objectives usually center on offsetting competitor promotions, building bank loyalty and gaining increased distribution coverage. Within the bank, objectives include preferential development of specific services, encouraging new account openings and cross-selling additional services.

10.4.2 The Choice of Promotional Tool

The tools available for achieving these objectives are many and varied. In choosing specific tools the bank should consider the market target, promotional objectives, likely competitive reactions and cost. The major tools available include the following.

1. *Samples, premiums and coupons.* Samples, widely used in consumer promotions, are normally more difficult to use in financial services where physical products rarely exist. Normally samples are therefore provided by offering customers free use of a service for a trial period to enable them to test

its value to them and to become familiar with its usage. Examples would include the offering of its Diners Club service by Citibank to new users free for six months; the provision of free corporate cash management interactive terminals to corporate treasurers for several months; and free home banking terminals for trial periods by a number of banks.

Premiums are products offered at a relatively low cost or free as an incentive to use a particular service. Premiums come in a wide variety of forms, and although the use of consumer appliances and the like as incentives for opening different levels of deposits which developed in the later 1970s when interest rates were controlled in the USA has diminished, they are still widely used. They include the provision of free T-shirts, specially shaped children's piggy banks, low-price telephones, home computers, book vouchers for students and the like. Coupons, which are certificates entitling the holder to a specific saving on a specific service, are not widely used in the banking industry. They are, however, effective in stimulating sales of new services and have been used to increase penetration in specific segments such as student, young people and senior citizen groups, where free banking services may be offered to new accounts. The travel and entertainment card concerns American Express and Diners Club also make extensive use of coupons as part of tie-in deals with restaurants and airlines to stimulate extra card usage.

2. *Point of sale displays and demonstrations.* Point of sale displays are used as silent salesmen in most bank branches. In general, however, such displays are weak and rely on impulse selection of bank service literature. This is often unattractive, being in leaflet form and rarely advertised to stimulate consumer awareness or interest. Demonstrations are, however, becoming much more important activities in bank marketing via the use of seminars and out-of-bank displays presented to focused corporate and individual customer groups. Professional demonstration teams and multimedia techniques are becoming common today and this area of activity is likely to increase in all market segments.

3. *Contests, sweepstakes and games.* The banking industry usually likes to consider itself above the use of such promotional devices. However, there is again growing employment of these tools to stimulate share and usage. For example, in the USA some banks have successfully endeavored to stimulate ATM usage by having customers record and submit transaction numbers as entries for sweepstakes. Others have developed contests for prizes in particular segments such as among young and senior citizen account holders. In the business market contests have also been use by Amex, again to stimulate card usage.

4. *Distribution system promotion.* Banks have used many techniques to stimulate the preferential use of their services with third parties. Tie-in

advertising allowances are common, especially by American Express, but also by other major card companies. Similarly Barclays, Citibank, American Express and others have provided special prices and allowances to participating banks distributing their travellers cheques. Credit finance subsidiaries of the banks have offered push money bonuses and contests to dealers to push their credit services. Specialty advertising items carrying the bank's logo such as pens, pencils and the like are commonplace. Some companies, notably American Express, will also reward account introductions by individuals with packs of wine and other free gifts. Overall, for services offered via third parties the banks have found it increasingly necessary to use sales promotion techniques to develop their market positions in the face of greater competition.

10.4.3 Developing Sales Promotion Programs

In designing the bank sales promotion program, determine the following:

1. Nature of audience participation. Decide precisely who the bank wishes to participate in the promotion and target on this customer segment.
2. Nature of incentive. Determine what form and size of incentive the bank should offer, aiming to establish one large enough to encourage the level of usage desired but bearing in mind that effectiveness diminishes beyond a certain point.
3. Nature of delivery system. Decide what delivery system the bank should use to disseminate the promotion. Each channel, branch, direct mail, press, in-store and the like will have different levels of reach and cost.
4. Duration of promotion. Ensure the length of time the promotion is offered is adequate for the selected audience to take advantage but still short enough not to lose impact.
5. Promotion timing. Most promotions are best undertaken at particular periods of the year. Thus home improvement loans might be best promoted in spring, student loans in the autumn.
6. Determine promotion budget. Normally sales promotion is treated as a component of the overall communications budget. The cost of individual promotions is calculated as the incentive cost multiplied by the expected usage plus the cost of administration. This can be compared with the expected gain in contribution from increased service usage.

10.4.4 Evaluating Promotion Performance

As a prelude to undertaking a full-scale promotion it is wise to attempt to pretest its effectiveness. Relatively few banks do this but alternative promotions can and should be tested in selected markets prior to any large-scale launch. Unfortunately, banks have a very bad history of post-promotion evaluation. It is, however, strongly recommended that such efforts are made.

At least banks should check the level of service utilization before, during and after a promotion. This latter should include both a short-term and a long-term effect measurement. Consumer panel data should be used to check the types of people who responded to a particular promotion and which ones remained affected over the long term. Finally, an attempt should be made to assess the overall effect on bank profitability of specific promotions.

10.4.5 Setting Public Relations Objectives

Specific objectives should be established for the public relations function so that the bank's money and effort is not dissipated over a wide spread of unfocused activities. Lloyds Bank, for example, has established a set of guidelines for its public relations with four main rules, namely:[1]

1. We do not sponsor individuals, only organizations
2. We do not put money into bricks and mortar
3. We do not support events outside the UK
4. We do not do any sport

The bank's reasons for these guidelines are that, as there are too many individuals to choose between it would be dysfunctional to make choices; bricks and mortar projects are not noticeable because they fail to involve people; sponsorship relates to the retail banking market which for Lloyds is largely in the UK; and sport is much too expensive for the bank's limited public relations budget. As a result the bank targets its activities very closely to specific groups such as the better educated young, farmers, young businessmen and the like. In its regional sponsorship the bank is looking mainly for opportunities for regional head offices and branches to combine customer entertainment with a demonstration of the bank's commitment to the community. As a result the bank is a strong supporter of agricultural shows, concerts and cultural events by touring national arts companies. Care should also be taken to link public relations strategy to overall communications policy. For example, the Midland Bank launched a major TV and press campaign to stress its friendliness and interest in customers under the theme of the 'listening bank'. However, when a number of press stories broke about court cases by the bank against individual customers who appeared to have overextended their credit positions this friendly image campaign looked like rebounding badly.

[1] *Lloyds Bank News* 1984, p. 5.

Strenuous public relations efforts were required to reduce the negative impact the court cases had on the overall effect of the campaign.

10.4.6 The Choice of Publicity Vehicles

The choice of suitable newsworthy, image-appropriate activities for the bank to engage in is critical to the success of public relations strategy. The public relations specialist is therefore interested in creating news rather than identifying it. The appropriate choice of events for support or sponsorship provides a vehicle to reach a variety of audiences with many stories. The wide variety of promotional opportunities arising from football sponsorship is illustrated below:[1]

— Providing tickets in a VIP box for good customers
— Sponsoring pre-and post-game receptions
— Using a coach or star as a spokesperson
— Developing point of sale materials and displays
— Providing schedules in a mailing
— Offering fan team shirts, photographs and the like
— Running advertising in scorecards and programmes
— Purchasing stadium advertising
— Circulating a highlight film in the offseason to clubs
— Recruiting and training a retired player to work
— Sponsoring half-time entertainment competitions
— Holding a lunch for key accounts with leading players at each table
— Sponsoring a young players' clinic
— Getting a top player to visit schools
— Arranging special seating for the handicapped at the stadium

10.4.7 Evaluating Public Relations Results

The precise measurement of the effect of public relations is difficult because it usually forms only a small part of the bank's overall communications strategy. One technique, which is not necessarily satisfactory, is to measure in terms of column inches of publication coupled with the circulation of these newspapers and magazines plus airtime and audience measures for TV and radio. While this physical measure monitors the level of exposure of the bank, it is also important to evaluate the changes in consumer attitudes, comprehension and attitude to the bank as a result of media exposure. This involves their measured evaluation before and after particular publicity campaigns. Finally, the overall profit impact should be measured wherever possible. This should be based on

[1] *ABA Banking Journal*, September 1984, p. 42.

the estimated effect of public relations on service performance. When estimated costs of providing the service have been deducted, the net contribution can be measured against direct costs of the publicity program to provide an estimated rate of return.

10.5 ADVERTISING

Advertising may be defined as a controlled form of non-personal presentation message about specific ideas or services from an identified sponsor via a specific communication medium designed to inform and persuade selected audiences to undertake actions desired by the sponsor. In recent years the role of advertising in the banking industry in both personal and corporate markets has expanded dramatically and the financial services industry is now one of the most important sources of advertising revenue. In developing advertising strategy the bank must first ensure that it conforms to overall marketing strategy. The process of developing advertising strategy then consists of the following steps:

— Set advertising objectives
— Establish copy platform
— Develop the media plan
— Set the advertising expenditure level
— Measure advertising effectiveness

10.5.1 Setting Advertising Objectives

Advertising objectives are generally identified as being of two types — direct action objectives, leading to measurable increases in variables such as sales or sales leads; and indirect action objectives aimed at communicating ideas and image and changing consumer habits, which affect sales in the long term. Both sets of objectives are usually difficult to measure objectively. Normally a mix of both direct and indirect objectives is adopted for the individual bank's advertising strategy. Popular advertising objectives include the following:

Induce trial. With new products or services' the advertising objective will be to induce trial. Ads will therefore tend to stress benefits coupled with coupons and free trial offers. For example Bank of America, to promote its home banking service, used a mixture of direct mail and press ads to sign 7500 participants with the inducement of three months free service if they signed within a set period.

Increase usage. Ads which encourage users to increase usage of bank services are designed in particular to promote the cross-selling of other services. Direct mail is especially useful for this type of advertising when services require regular mailings such as statements. Barclay Card therefore uses its monthly mailings to promote a series of other services such as personal and household insurance and personal loans. A Midland Bank campaign which demonstrates the wide variety of uses to which personal loans can be put similarly encourages increased service usage.

Build differentiation. Much advertising is designed to build differentiation between banks. Some such advertising is image-generating, such as that of J. P. Morgan, which emphasizes its strength in depth in providing large multinationals with specialized services. By contrast, Citibank has built its differentiation around its electronic banking skills, using ads to stress its position as the 'citi of tomorrow'.

Confirm image. Many ads are aimed at providing confirmation of a bank's image. Thus Trustee Savings Bank ads stress that the bank is a consumer oriented institution and is the bank 'that likes to say yes'.

Change behavior. Advertising can be used to help change people's behavior. Citibank has used advertising to help sell the concept of 24 hour cash availability via ATMs; similarly in the corporate market the bank emphasizes the value of speed in its ad to change corporate treasurers over to using global electronic banking rather than paper-based systems.

Increase awareness. Such campaigns are designed to demonstrate and to remind customers that specific banks can and do provide specific services. The Bank of Boston thus stresses that it not only has an extensive international network but also knows the local banking markets in the 38 countries in which it operates. Many geographic specialist banks around the world adopt similar awareness campaigns to encourage correspondent bank and foreign business.

Generate sales leads. The objective of such ads is usually centered on obtaining names of prospective customers. In banking relatively few ads generate leads by offering inducements but rather aim to provide additional information. Business expansion scheme ads from a number of banks and investment houses in the UK illustrate sales lead ads. They are also commonly used in corporate bank advertising, where individuals are nominated to receive suitable incoming enquiries.

Increase sales. An advertising objective which leads to a direct increase in sales is highly desirable. Relatively few campaigns enable such an objective to be immediately achieved. Typical campaigns where such an effect can be demonstrated tend to be press or direct mail dominated, such as the development of money fund deposits in the United States.

Build image. The demonstration of ambiance in an ad campaign helps to build image irrespective of actual costs. Thus Visa, Mastercard and American Express stress the added features and relative exclusivity of their gold card products by demonstrating their use in exclusive locations.

Provide information. Many ads are designed to demonstrate how a service actually works. This is especially true of complex services such as the Merrill Lynch CMA ads, which endeavor to stress the comprehensiveness of the service being offered.

10.5.2 Establishing Copy Platform

Having established the objectives of advertising strategy, it is important next to establish what an ad should say. A review of the product attributes and benefits together with an assessment of consumer needs should establish the foundation for developing the copy platform. This is a critical element in designing ad strategy and such platforms incorporate the following features:[1]

1. *Principal product benefits*
   (a) The big advantage
       (i) Exclusivity points
       (ii) Differentiating points
   (b) Secondary advantages
       (i) Quality features
       (ii) Quality workmanship
2. *Ad objectives*
   (a) Desired initial response from prospect
   (b) Desired future behavior of prospect
3. *Creative tasks*
   (a) Selling theme
   (b) Verbal approach
   (c) Visual approach

Once the overall platform has been established the copywriter has a number of further decisions to make:

---

[1] W. K. Hafer and G. E. White, *Advertising Writing,* West Publishing Co., p. 48.

— To determine the format of the ad
— To structure the ad
— To set the ad style

Copy format. Having decided upon what the ad platform should be, the next step is to determine which to select from among the choice of copy formats open to the copywriter. The copy format establishes the way in which the ad message will be presented. Major formats include the following:

Testimonial—the ad message in this format is presented as a testimonial by a client stressing the benefits of working with the bank. Chase Manhattan's campaign stressing the theme of the 'Chase Partnership' illustrates such a format, with companies such as Parfums Christian Dior acting as testimonials.

Humorous—not used heavily in the banking industry for corporate markets, humor has been used more commonly in retail markets. Funny ads do not necessarily sell services, however, even though they may have high awareness and retention characteristics. An example of such a campaign is the National Westminster Bank cinema campaign on the opening of a bank account by a punk youth, which stresses that bank accounts are not restricted to upper class citizens.

Cartoons—cartoon formats are often used in combination with humor and may be employed by banks to lower their forbidding image. The use of a cartoon version of the Midland Bank's Griffin corporate identity in its listening bank campaign illustrates this.

Straight sell—Ads using a straight sell format stress the expected conscumer benefits and aim for direct action. The Trustee Savings Bank home contents insurance services campaign illustrates such a format. The ad stresses the dangers of burglary and the benefits of TSB cover; it ends with an application form to complete including a table enabling the applicant to calculate the precise premium to be paid for a particular level of cover.

News—such a format reads like a magazine story and gives the impression of being part of the newspaper or magazine in which it is contained. News ads tend to generate high readership levels because of their format.

Educational—this copy format is used to stress corporate services to create primary demand or to provide information about a product. The 'citi of tomorrow' campaign illustrates how Citibank's worldwide electronic banking services can be employed to solve complex problems by using the bank's advanced technology.

In addition to the choice of format, the size, color and visual content of an ad can dramatically affect its appeal as well as its cost. Larger ads do gain more attention but this is not necessarily proportional to the addition in cost.

Copy structure. Irrespective of copy format, the critical task of an ad is to be structured to gain the attention of the audience to which it is directed. Traditionally, the content of well-structured ads should reflect AIDA, standing for Attention, Interest, Desire, Action.

The first task of the ad is to create attention. For press ads this is critically determined by the use of visuals and headlines. For TV the storyboard is important. In practice many bank ads are boring, being weak in attention and interest and totally lacking in the ability to develop desire and action. Some ads tend to be more designed to placate internal management desires for image rather than to sell. Despite the massive growth in ad spend therefore, relatively few financial service industry campaigns have been memorable.

The second task of the ad is to generate interest. While the headline and visual are used to gain attention, the first paragraph of an ad should stress the important benefits that can be expected from using the service. The body of the copy aims to create desire while the closing part of the ad should generate action. Many bank ads fail to close, and omit to provide a contact point where the potential client can satisfy any aroused desire. Additional maxims for good advertising are that ad copy should be believable, retain simplicity and be readable. Successful ads should also possess good stopping power as a result of their visuals and headline; should have strong, powerful headlines; make significant promises; be persuasive; create a positive feeling; and be distinctive relative to competitive offerings.[1] Banks should judge their ad campaigns with these concepts in mind.

10.5.3 Media Planning

Media planning is concerned with identifying the most cost-effective way of delivering the desired number of ad exposures to a target audience, bearing in mind also the competitive traffic aimed at the same audience. Key factors which influence the media plan include the following:

Advertising budget. The size of the ad budget is a critical determination in media planning since certain media will be excluded or reduced as a result of time and space costs. The cost of specific media will also be affected by the discount structure they offer.

Media Reach. Each medium has its own specific audience. The media planner must identify from this audience how well the specific medium

[1] Richard C. Christian. Stopping power: one of six characteristics of great ads. *Marketing News* **14**, No. 6 (February 6, 1981), p. 18.

reaches the target audience he is interested in, since rates will not normally be related to this group but rather to the coverage as a whole.

Media availability. Not all media are available in all markets. Media plans must therefore take account both of specific media and of time and space slots which might be desired for particular campaigns.

Competition. Media plans should take into account the activities of competitors and endeavor to differentiate from these, although similar media should be used if these are seen as traditional. Specialist agencies such as Leading National Advertisers in the USA and MEAL in the UK respectively provide detailed analysis of competitive media usage.

Relative dominance. The relative weight of advertising a particular advertiser can bring to a medium compared with competitors is an indication of its ability to dominate or be dominated. Obviously, awareness and impact will be significantly affected by ad relative weight and media planners should ensure that this will be strong enough to achieve overall advertising objectives.

Today media planning models are commonly used to optimize the choice of specific media to reach given target audiences with the desired frequency. The advantages and disadvantages of particular media are summarized in Figure 10.4. The use of broadcast media by banks has grown substantially in recent years although in the United States the regionalization of banking has tended to militate against national broadcast campaigns. In countries allowing nationwide branching, however, TV and radio for retail and mortgage banking services have become the main media used. Press is still used heavily and has grown in real terms in line with the overall rise in bank advertising. It has been found especially important in the growth of direct response retail services, notably for the sale of savings and insurance products. Corporate service advertising has tended to stress press, with financial journals, the specialist international financial press and general business magazines being the major media. Direct marketing has also grown in importance for both retail and corporate banking services. Point of sale is used in branches but has not been developed to a significant degree, while outdoor media have not been heavily used by banks except for promotion purposes.

10.5.4 Setting the Advertising Appropriation

Many bank advertising campaigns have been badly conceived and conducted in a haphazard manner at great cost. The advertising appropriation decision and the allocation of these funds to specific campaigns need to be carefully determined and the rationale for the decisions established as part of the bank's overall marketing program. Unfortunately, there is no clearly superior method

	Newspapers	Magazines	Radio	TV	Direct mail	Point of purchase
Advantages	Geographic selectivity	Demographic selectivity	Geographic/demographic selectivity	Show & tell	Selectivity	Longevity
	Flexibility	Permanence	Flexibility	Geographic selectivity	Permanence	Flexibility
	Editorial support	High-quality presentation	Cheap	Penetration	Flexibility	Selectivity
	Secondary readership	Editorial support			Impact	
	Cooperative advertising	Secondary readership			Measureability	
Disadvantages	Lack of permanence	Lack of flexibility	Perishability	Perishability	Cost	Limited space
	Poor quality	Limited availability	Cluttered	Cost	Lack of editorial support	Ad costs
	Limited demographic orientation	Expensive	Lack of visual support	Cluttered	Lack of reader influence	
			Use as background medium			

Figure 10.4   Advantages and disadvantages of specific media

Source: Derived from: William H. Bolen, Advertising 2nd Edition, John Wiley, 1984

of fixing these sums. In practice a variety of methods are in use. The main such methods include the following:

Percentage of deposits method. A popular method used by a substantial number of organizations checks the bank's level of advertising spend against that of other comparable banks and companies' relative levels of deposit bases. Thus if the industry average ad spend is 0.2 per cent of deposits this sets the level of appropriation for the bank.

Care must be taken in the use of this method since it may not be an appropriate one in achieving desired marketing strategy outcomes. It is popular, however, due to its simplicity and because as deposits rise so too does advertising appropriation.

Match competitors method. A second method used occasionally sets advertising spend to match that of competitors. The banking industry, with its strong follow-the-leader tendency, has tended to watch competitor spend levels closely and maintain relative parity. One peculiar result of this form of advertising is the heavy weight of appropriation used to create ads such as tombstones placed in journals largely read by other bankers as distinct from a strong readership of potential clients.

What you can afford method? A number of banks, notably smaller ones, decide on an advertising appropriation based upon what they believe they can afford. The determination of this amount is, however, obviously subjective.

Market share method. In order to increase market share, some banks attempt to spend more than their relative market share position would suggest. There has been some empirical evidence to suggest that a correlation exists betwen market share and share of advertising. However, this does not consider advertising quality, the role of advertising in the marketing mix or the role of other marketing factors. For example, the Midland Bank launched a heavy corporate advertising campaign which stressed the bank's international services and challenged potential customers to test the bank to deliver. This campaign was run with a relative ad weight several times that of Midland's interest rivals but failed to substantially shift the bank's image among large multinationals.

Objective and task method. This method is different to those discussed above as the appropriation is developed based on the procedure of first setting marketing objectives; followed by advertising objectives and media plans to achieve a specific task. This is the approach that emerges by following the model developed at the beginning of this chapter. The task method assesses what is needed to achieve objectives, thereby reducing potential for wastage or forcing the revision of objectives if adequate funds are not available. Relatively few organizations use this method, however, and it is still subjectively dependent upon the choice of appropriate objectives and the correct understanding of the linkage between these objectives and the selected media plan and copy platform.

Quantitative models. A number of quantitative modelling methods have been reported to determine the optimal advertising appropriation.[1] These methods have found little use at present in the banking industry.

There is no best method of determining the size of the advertising appropriation. In most banks it would be appropriate to make use of a combination of several of the above methods. These should include a task oriented approach together with qualitative methods which take account of competitive actions and also what the bank can afford.

10.5.5 Measuring Advertising Effectiveness

In a recent study of 300 US banks and financial services companies,[2] the Financial Research Council, a subsidiary of the Advertising Research Foundation, found that the companies had little knowledge of the effectiveness of their advertising expenditure. Specific findings included the fact that little research was conducted prior to ad campaigns to adequately define market boundaries or assess customer needs. Second, there was little commitment to research designed to evaluate advertising before major expenditures were made. Third, the banks did not have strong in-house skills to conduct research nor did they use external organizations effectively. Finally, as a result, four out of ten respondents did not conduct any advertising research at all. Given the rapid rise in advertising expenditure by banks, this failure to evaluate the effects of such expenditures is dangerous and should be corrected.

Most work actually undertaken is concerned with the pretesting of given ads rather than post-evaluation. Where post-evaluation is conducted, most advertisers try to measure the indirect objective effects on awareness, image and preference. Direct objective effects tend to be more difficult to measure except for direct response and direct mail advertising.

Pretesting of ads is undertaken before actual media expenditure is committed. There are three main methods used, namely:[3]

[1] Gary L. Lillen and P. Kotler, *Marketing Decision Making,* Harper and Row, New York, 1983, pp. 492–501.
[2] *ABA Banking Journal,* October 1983, p. 31.
[3] P. Kotler, *Marketing Management,* 5th edn., Prentice Hall, London, 1984, pp. 655–656.

Direct ratings. A method which asks a selected panel of consumers exposed to alternative ad's to rate them in order of preference. Ads may also be rated according to their attention, readthrough, cognitive affective and behavioral strengths.

Portfolio tests. In this method consumers are asked to look through a portfolio of ads and are then questioned, either aided or unaided, on their ability to recall specific ads and their content. This suggests a measure of an individual ads ability to stand out and its message to be retained and understood.

Laboratory tests. Some researchers use instruments to measure physiological reactions to an ad. These tests mainly measure the attention-getting power.

Ad post-testing methods include:

Recall tests. Researchers test consumers who have been exposed to ads to recall ads and copy themes. Such recall scores measure impact and memorability.

Recognition tests. In this method readers of a magazine, for example, are given particular issues and asked to point out what they recognize. These tests enable advertisers to compare their ads' impact with those of competitors.

Sales effect measurement is harder. It is most difficult to measure in corporate image-building advertising. Researchers do try to measure effectiveness through historical and experimental analysis techniques. Historical analysis usually correlates past sales with past advertising expenditure on a current or lagged basis using various statistical techniques. With experimental designs, particular campaign ad weights can be tested against specific sales levels achieved to assess relative weight effectiveness.

10.6 SUMMARY

The emergence of communications as a critical ingredient in bank marketing strategy means that a professional approach must be adopted to the integrated management of this function. The roles of the relevant elements in the communications mix between personal selling, promotion and public relations and advertising need to be carefully identified and modified if necessary in line with changing marketing strategy. This is especially true as the cost of providing personal selling increases in retail and corporate banking market segments.

For each element of the communications mix, objectives need to be developed. These objectives should be achieved by an appropriate choice of policy. The results from adopting specific policies should be carefully monitored and if necessary the mix or the objectives should be modified to ensure the strategy is both internally consistent and achievable.

10.7 COMMUNICATIONS STRATEGY CHECKLIST

Use the following checklist to evaluate your bank's communications strategy:

1. Does your bank communications strategy specifically identify who you wish to communicate with, where, when, how often and by what means?
2. Does it also estimate at what cost and what the expected results should be?
3. Is the role of personal selling clearly identified for each customer segment?
4. Have you evaluated whether traditional personal selling methods are still appropriate? Is the role of the branch manager in particular clearly identified?
5. Have you introduced suitable sales training programs to reeducate and improve the selling skills of branch staff? Is your reward system appropriate to the achievement of personal selling objectives?
6. Have you explored the use of specialist personal selling teams such as account executives for both corporate and high net worth personal clients?
7. Have you tested seminar selling, telemarketing and other more efficient uses of personal selling?
8. Has your bank established suitable objectives for its sales promotion activities?
9. Have sales promotion methods been adopted which support these objectives?
10. Have you developed appropriate sales promotion programs and the means of evaluating them?
11. Has your bank established suitable objectives for your public relations activities?
12. Has the appropriate choice of publicity vehicles been made to fulfil these objectives?
13. Have you established appropriate means of evaluating the results of your public relations efforts?
14. Has your bank set out clear objectives for its advertising communications?
15. Have you estalished appropriate copy platforms for your advertising?

Do your ads possess AIDA and conform to other successful ad style elements?

16. Have you made adequate allowance to pretest your ads for qualitative content to check their ability to create awareness, interest, desire and action?

17. Have you effectively evaluated competitor advertising against your own?

18. Has media planning been undertaken to identify the most cost-effective way of reaching your desired audience with the planned number of exposures?

19. Have you evaluated the alternative media choices available in terms of their advantages and disadvantages and your specific communication message needs?

20. Have you developed a logical advertising appropriation budget taking into account the task of your advertising and competitor actions?

21. Have you developed ways of testing your advertising effectiveness both in terms of direct and indirect objective effects?

CHAPTER 11

Bank Organization Structure

11.1 INTRODUCTION

A key factor which differentiates banks in servicing the markets in which they operate and a crucial element in successful strategy implementation is the form of organization adopted. Some structures do appear more appropriate than others in serving particular markets, but history and the nature of the bank's core business tend to significantly influence the form of organization adopted for other markets. These differences can thus provide a particular bank with a specific advantage or disadvantage. While the overall administrative requirements of the bank must be taken into account therefore, it is important to bear in mind that under normal circumstances the requirements of particular customer clusters should receive priority.

11.2 FORMS OF BANK ORGANIZATION

As banks have developed differently in different countries and states due largely to regulatory variations several particular bank organizational models have emerged. The major organization forms that can be identified are as follows:

11.2.1 Retail/Commerical Branch Based Structure

This is found commonly in many European banks where countrywide branching is permissible and where early development usually centered upon retail/small business transaction based banking. During the 1960s and 1970s these banks expanded their international branch coverage, the activity of which was usually more wholesale/corporate in orientation. In addition they usually diversified their product range both domestically and internationally into related banking services, notably credit finance and leasing. The structure of these banks emphasizes organization by geography, based historically upon the structure used to manage the local branch network. Related banking

200

services are seldom integrated within mainstream bank operations but are organized as loosely coordinated separate subsidiaries. Many such banks have recently developed key account units for major corporate customers whose brief is to provide a global account officer and international coordination crossing the normal geographic divisional boundaries. However, profit responsibility is usually left with the regional units. Examples of banks like this would include Barclays, Lloyds and AmRo Bank. Details of this type of structure are shown in Figure 11.1.

11.2.2 Customer/Service Based Structure

Many US banks with limited local state branching capability have organized with structures based around customer clusters. These banks have primarily focused upon corporate accounts and have relatively small retail businesses. They tend to organize around local banking and international operations, with the latter being primarily concerned with large corporations. Locally the focus will be retail banking, local metro-business and out-of-state US corporate banking. Corporate banking is therefore handled at the level of the branch for very small business, with geographic account officer structures dealing with middle market accounts and industry specialization being quite common for large corporate acounts. International activities tend to be organized largely on a geographic regional basis, but below this level in large branches and in the USA customer structuring by industry specialization is also common. Many such banks also have a key multinational account unit responsible for servicing around 500 or so major global MNCs. Related banking services, trust and investment services tend to be organized firstly by function and separately from retail and commercial banking. Such banks tend to have only limited retail aspirations away from their local geographic areas although many have offered high net worth private banking as a special service for a limited number of individual accounts. Examples of such structures would include Continental Illinois, Chemical New York Corpn and Manufacturers Hanover. Details of this type of structure are shown in Figure 11.2.

11.2.3 Customer Based Structure

A recent adaptation of the customer/service based system is the customer based structure where, for example, the bank has clustered all its relevant services for a particular customer group under the same global organization. Thus all consumer banking services around the world ultimately report to the head of consumer banking. Similarly, corporate or institutional banking incorporates all the bank's services designed to service the corporate market, including activities such as asset based finance which are more commonly handled by separate subsidiaries. Omitted from such structures are merchant banking and investment and trust services, which together with international

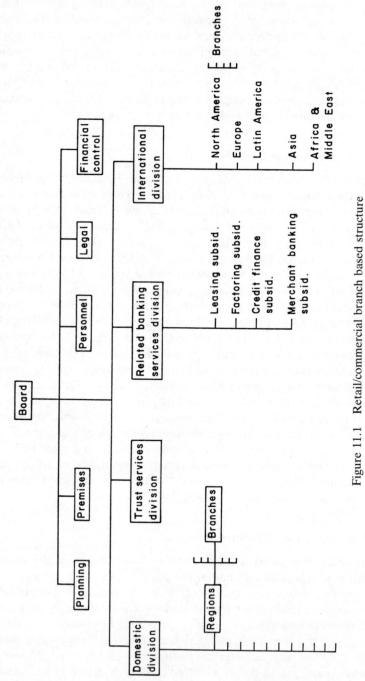

Figure 11.1   Retail/commercial branch based structure

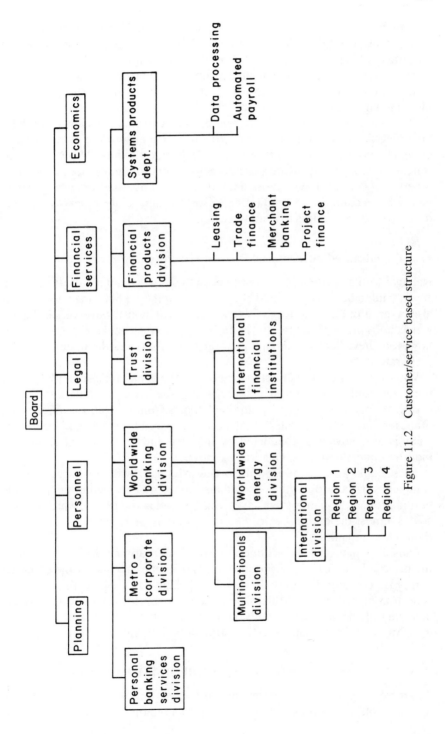

Figure 11.2 Customer/service based structure

private banking and securities information and dealing are tending to be brought into capital markets groups. Further, banks adopting this structure may have segregated systems based products as separate product based units covering retail, correspondent and institutional banking. Examples of this form of organization are Citicorp and Chase Manhattan and the structure is illustrated in Figure 11.3.

Different banks emphasize different product customer segments and these are reflected in their organizational structures. Some therefore place a greater or lesser emphasis on retail or wholesale business. Some like Citicorp or Barclays endeavor to provide a comprehensive level of international coverage, others like J. P. Morgan a more limited degree of overseas branching. Some banks have emphasized credit finance or leasing, while others have only developed these services to a limited extent.

11.2.4 Centralized International Division Structure

Relative to the position in Western banks the large commercial city banks in Japan tend to be less diversified both in terms of the service range offered and also in terms of loan maturity. This is a function of industry structure in Japan, which limits the deposit type and maturity open to such banks. By comparison, however, these banks, although providing retail services, lend mainly to the corporate sector.

While operating through a branch network, the banks are also subdivided by both geography and industry in servicing the corporate market. Large customers may be serviced by account officers from the central office while branches look after smaller local accounts. Credit review and economic analysis are, however, conducted by industry and a very detailed level of industry understanding is the norm.

These banks are also the central short-term funds provider to a large group of companies based around the old Zaibatsu concept or formed in the post-war period around the banks themselves. Such an industrial group, which usually covers almost the entire spectrum of the economy, may well embrace over a thousand companies.

Outside Japan these banks operate *via* an international division, although the principal contact with domestic based companies occurs *via* the domestic corporate banking divisions. In decision-making Japanese banks operate a consensus approach, with loans being decided by a formal 'Ringi' system involving all relevant departments. Discretion limits at individual units are thus low. An example of a Japanese-type structure is illustrated in Figure 11.4.

11.3 ORGANIZING FOR CORPORATE BANKING

Apart from service range, branch network cover and nationality, one of the most notable competitive differences observed amongst banks is the way in

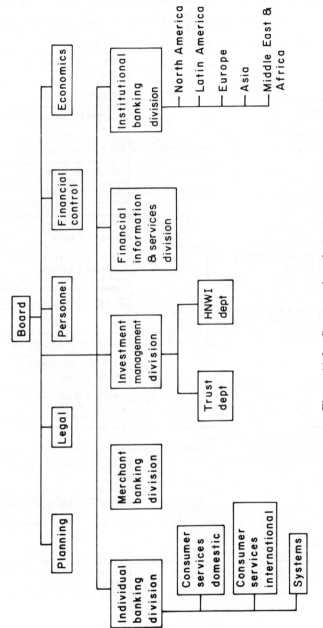

Figure 11.3   Customer based structure

206

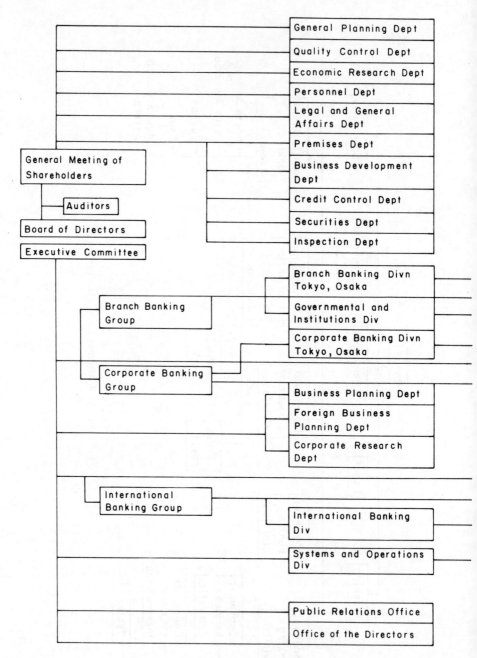

Figure 11.4 Centralized international division structure. *Source: Corporate records*

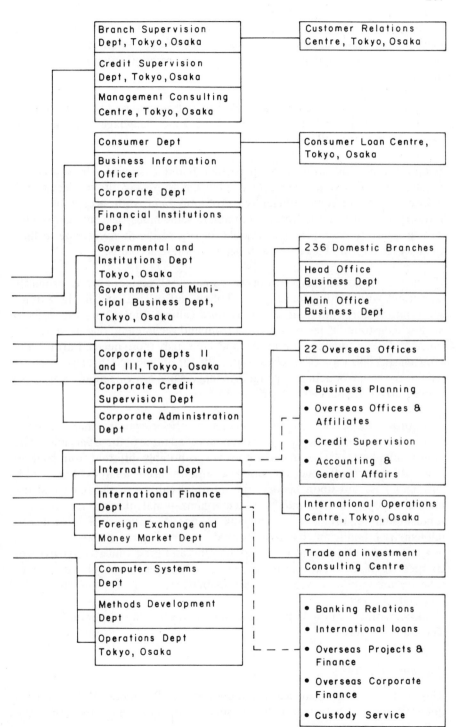

which they organize their marketing and selling effort for the corporate market. In organizing to service the corporate market a number of variables have to be carefully balanced. In particular, organization structures must take account of:

Geography This variable plays a major role in branch based banking systems and in international banking, where time zone, language, currency and national boundaries all influence structure.

Industry Many industries have particular banking service needs which it requires specialist skills to deliver if a bank is to manage its services to the industry competitively, efficiently, profitably and with acceptable risk. Industry specialists are therefore common in some industries and many banks now use industry as a primary variable for organizing their customer calling capacity for large and even medium sized corporate accounts.

Product The days when corporate commercial bankers were primarily concerned with lending have gone. Today and increasingly in the future, servicing the corporate market will require calling officers with the skills to analyse a customer's needs and select from and recommend one or more of a range of diverse financial service products to satisfy those needs. Further, the growing specialization of services, especially for off balance sheet products, is leading to the introduction of product managers in a growing number of banks in order to ensure balance in marketing effort.

In order to service many segments of the corporate market, bank organizations will need to integrate elements of all three of these variables. The relative emphasis placed on each, however, is notably different from bank to bank. Often such differences are not based upon a careful analysis of the bank's customer base but upon history, the informal culture of the bank and the maintenance of the *status quo* by vested organizational interests. It is usually a fundamental requirement that a bank change its structure if it wishes to implement a significant change in its mode of servicing the corporate market, as was recently the case at Chase Manhattan and First Chicago. Analysis of competitive bank organization can be an extremely powerful indicator of relative strength and weakness in capability to service segments of the corporate market.

Six main organizational forms are common for servicing corporate accounts. These are as follows:

Account executive

This is the system historically adopted by US commercial banks both domestically and internationally to service medium and large corporate accounts. An individual officer or coordinated group of individual officers is responsible for servicing a particular account domestically or globally. These officers, while taking account of geography, tend to be primarily concerned with accounts drawn from a specific industry or industries. Where accounts cross territorial boundaries, global account officers may also be appointed responsible for managing or coordinating a team of local field account officers each of whom services a specific unit or group of units of a large, usually geographically diversified account. The account executive structure developed in banks where retail branches were relatively rare and where the banks therefore relied more on servicing specific corporate accounts rather than individual consumers. A cutoff clearly exists at which time it becomes preferable to service accounts at the branch level, but most US banks will use direct calling officers for medium size accounts with a turnover of say more than $10 million per annum. Some have also opened corporate branches to provide a specialized service to accounts with a turnover substantially below this figure.

Relationship manager

The modern variant of the account executive is the relationship manager. Banks with account executive structures have been increasing the responsibilities of their account officers as they have expanded their product range. The relationship manager is seen as the principal interface between the bank and its customer. He is expected to possess sufficient product knowledge to provide a comprehensive level of service to the account and be able to diagnose customer needs sufficiently to recognize when and what specialist skills are required to supplement his own knowledge.

Branch manager

This was the system historically operated by banks in countries or states allowing branch banking. The local branch manager was traditionally responsible for servicing all the accounts within the geographic boundaries of his branch with all the bank's products. Where corporate accounts might have operations in several branch territories or overseas, integration of bank services was largely informal.

Corporate branches

A recent variation of the branch manager system has removed responsibility for larger accounts from local branches and concentrated it in a regional corporate branch where specialist corporate bankers look after the affairs of institutional customers only. Integration between regions and internationally in such structures tends to remain informal.

Mixed systems

A further variation of the branch manager system involves the use of bank directors and/or account executives to provide a coordination role for very large dispersed accounts in conjunction with branch manager and/or corporate branches. The location of the coordinating role varies according to account size and may be at regional or head office level.

Product managers

As corporate banking has increased in complexity, the dominating position of lending as the key task of the account executive has changed. In particular, new products and services have been added to the portfolio of corporate bankers which have been developed outside the line credit function. The new systems products have notably emerged from operations. In order to provide added impetus to the marketing of these new services a growing number of banks are appointing product managers charged with developing marketing plans for the products/services under their control. Some are actually going to the point of creating new profit center divisions concerned with systems products.

11.3.1 The Branch Manager System

The traditional use of branch managers in many European banks to service corporate accounts is being shown to be impracticable. The task of the branch manager in providing an adequate level of corporate service is almost impossible, since he must act as:

— administrator of his branch;
— a principal reference point for personal banking services;
— a salesman for an increasing range of non-banking services;
— a specialist corporate banker.

At the same time, the branch manager rarely has sufficient lending discretion to adequately meet the needs of even medium-sized accounts. He therefore runs the risk of being perceived as a form of 'messenger' rather than as a responsible executive.

The branch manager system is not without advantages, however, including the following:

— Branch managers are generally very experienced practical bankers and are trained as generalists.
— While lacking in some aspects of credit evaluation, they are generally more skilled than young account executives at personal evaluation.

The corporate branch system also gets around many of the negative aspects of the traditional branch system and is well suited to handle middle market accounts. Thus, coupled with industry specialized large corporate account bankers operating from national or regional centers, European bankers have substantially improved their capability to handle corporate accounts.

11.3.2 The Account Officer System

As a result of competitive pressures European banks have moved more towards account officer systems similar to those used by the US banks. The account officer is expected to:

— find his own customers;
— be responsible for the whole relationship with a customer, including the recommendation of a facility, negotiating its details and the loan agreement where relevant, following up the loan and the customer to ensure both remain sound;
— understand the customer's needs and problems and be able to provide help and guidance;
— familiarize himself with the customer's industry and with his customer's customers and suppliers;
— be constantly seeking new opportunities to provide additional services up to the credit levels deemed desirable;
— maintain and update his account plans and strategy by continuously seeking new information and financial analysis of the ongoing situation;
— constantly monitor and record competitive activity at his accounts;
— be fully responsible within the bank for his own lending recommendations and subsequent follow-up;
— unlike the traditional branch manager, be wholly dedicated to a relatively small number of corporate accounts.

The US bank mode of corporate servicing, although possessing advantages over the conventional branch manager system, is not without disadvantages:

— Account officer systems are expensive.
— Coordination for accounts utilizing many bank branches/territories may not be good.
— Account officers are usually trained as lending officers, and as a consequence tend to be loan volume oriented and have weak non-loan product knowledge.
— Account officers may block or deter the development of non-loan, fee-based products because they do not have adequate knowledge to recognize and recommend help for specialist service needs at an account.

— US banks particularly tend to be somewhat parochial in their view of the world. For example, they tend to see other US banks abroad as their principal competitors in overseas markets despite the fact that any increase in market penetration normally comes from indigenous banks. This parochialism tends to infiltrate into the account officer force, even though many will be non-US nationals.
— Many banks use relatively young and inexperienced bankers as account officers. Further, they change them frequently, so making relationship building especially difficult.

The account executive system tends to provide a much more detailed (and expensive) level of service to corporate accounts. To recover its cost good penetration and a high volume of profitable business is important. This mode of servicing, therefore, should normally not be used below medium sized accounts where a minimum call rate of four per year for an active account is profitably sustainable.

11.3.3 The Relationship Manager System

An increasing number of banks are now moving toward a relationship manager system for servicing large corporate accounts. The key global officer is identified as the primary contact point within the bank for the corporate customer and the officer himself is expected to be able to introduce all the bank's mainline services. While the relationship manager is not expected to be fully aware of the details of the entire range of bank services, he is expected to be a generalist banker rather than being primarily oriented to lending. To help build such long-term relationships some banks are keeping the same relationship managers in an account for a considerable number of years. In this way they hope to avoid the criticism concerning young, inexperienced and frequently changing account officers leveled at many banks.

The relationship manager system is also not without problems. Firstly, the conversion of specialist lending oriented bankers to generalists is difficult and the organizational culture of many banks makes this transition doubly difficult. Secondly, a very substantial improvement in both bank product knowledge and corporate needs identification is required of traditional lending officers.

11.4 ASSESSING ACCOUNT OFFICER NEEDS

The cost of servicing corporate accounts can be very high, depending upon the type of calling system used, and the level of calling intensity will be related to the size and scale of business at the individual account. When assessing the resource requirement for a particular business development approach, the following factors need to be taken into account.

— How many calls can your account executive/branch managers make a year? This will depend upon the size of accounts called upon and the degree of activity at each one.

— What is the cost of their operation and how does this translate in costs per call? This is usually high, and management time can be usefully devoted to reducing costs per call by increasing call rates and/or cutting operating costs.

— How many times do you think accounts should be called on and how much business must be generated to cover these costs? As part of the account planning process calculate the approximate breakeven per account even when a strong account based financial control system is not in place.

— How many accounts are there where the available potential permits you to expect to recover your costs? Remember when assessing account potential that it is that business you have a reasonable ability to win that is relevant.

— What is the total number of new/existing business calls you need to make on these accounts?

— Does the presently available/planned call capacity match the number required?

— If not, what management action is required?

— For multisite accounts, what coordination mechanisms have been built in to ensure overall adequate calling/servicing/information inter-change/account planning?

The account planning process is discussed in detail in Chapter 6.

11.5 SPECIALIZED ORGANIZATIONAL SKILLS

Today many banks have added a series of specialized skill areas which may operate in either a line or account manager staff support capacity. With the division of banks into strategic business units such organizational groups are tending to become line profit centers. These are usually designed to attack particular customer/product segments. The most common such specialist organizational units are as follows.

11.5.1 Large Multinational Corporation Accounts

Most major commercial banks have a target or hit list of large worldwide MNCs which are considered to be priority accounts for the bank. Such hit lists usually identify around 500 accounts, and although a jealously guarded secret, tend in about 80 per cent of cases to duplicate the hit lists of other major banks. However, all the banks are distinctively *not* the same in their capability to service these accounts. As a result many banks have found it difficult to penetrate them profitably. An increasing number of banks are therefore questioning their large corporate strategies and turning more to serving smaller accounts.

In servicing such accounts a coordinated team approach is necessary since the account, while based in one country, may require services in many markets around the world. In 1974, for example, Citicorp established its World Corporation Group to service some 450 global MNCs, about half of which were based *outside* the USA. Each of these accounts was assigned an account executive responsible for dealing with the organization headquarters in whatever country it might be located. This executive was held profit accountable for the client and was manager of a group of 20–30 account officers assigned to manage profitably the affairs of each company in their own countries. Each officer handled a mix of, on average, between eight and ten accounts, in some cases dealing with the parent company treasury and in others with a purely local subsidiary or division treasury. Similarly, each account officer prepared account plans each year against which he was measured in terms of personal performance.

In 1980 Citicorp restructured its World Corporation Group and extended its global account coverage to around 2500 accounts making up the bulk of the corporate loan portfolio. Each such account was profit planned, with the global account officer being responsible for the overall plan and individual country based executives responsible for their subcomponent of the account plan. Progress against plan was closely monitored by an account based control system which measured return on total assets (including committed rather than merely outstanding lines). Such a customer based system also potentially allows the allocation of country limit to the account rather than leaving this solely to the discretion of country managers. An example of a multinational corporation specialist service unit is shown in Figure 11.5.

By comparison relatively few European banks provide this level of global service and seldom effectively coordinate their calling efforts on a worldwide basis. Moreover, such banks have rarely developed the specialized products and services needed by such accounts. Even many US banks do not offer the same level of coordinated calling effort for MNC accounts, hence Citicorp and a few other US banks have achieved a high level of account penetration in such accounts around the world. By comparison, even within Europe, the leading European banks have achieved only limited market penetration outside their indigenous home market.

11.5.2 Project Finance

A second area of recent specialization has been that of large-scale project finance. In some banks project finance is dealt with within merchant banking subsidiaries, while in others it remains within the commercial bank organization.

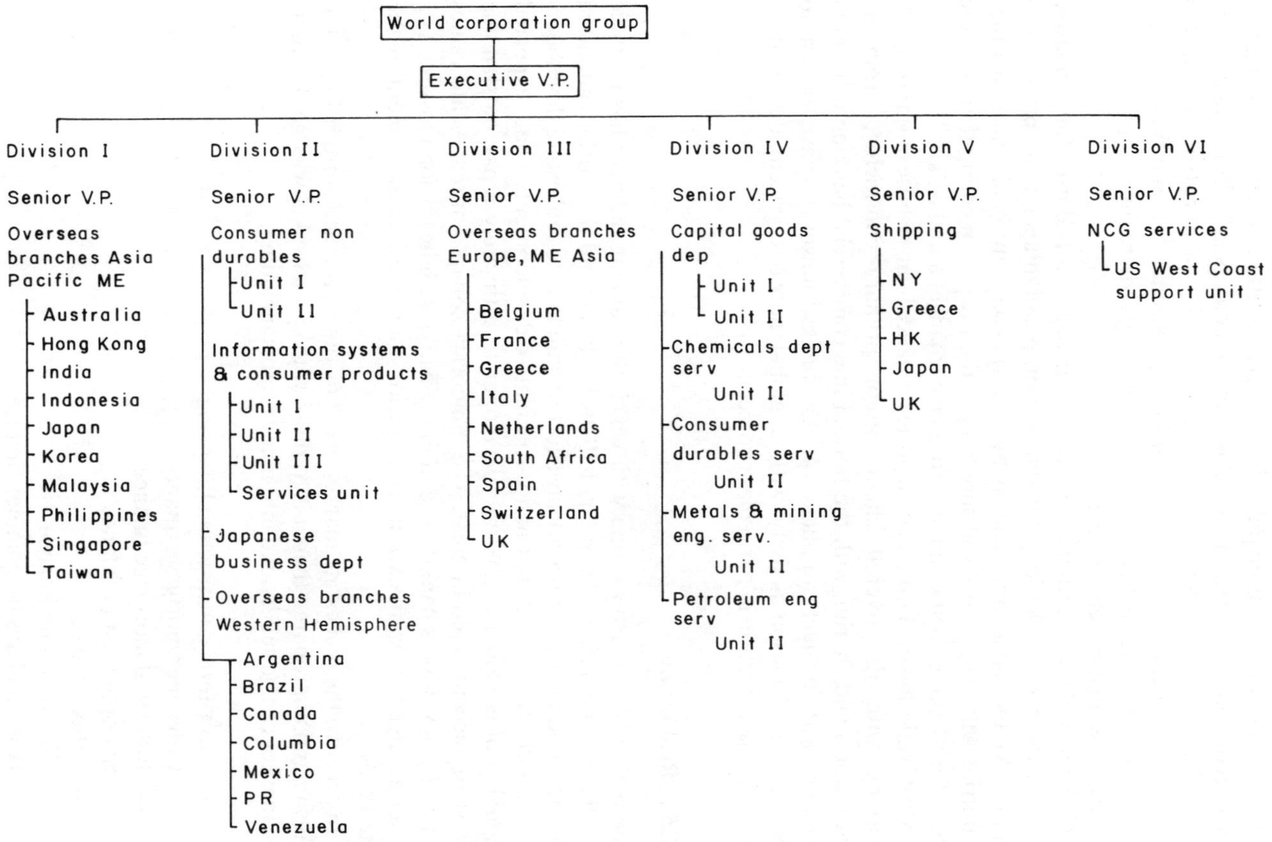

World corporation group

Executive V.P.

Division I
Senior V.P.

Overseas branches Asia Pacific ME
- Australia
- Hong Kong
- India
- Indonesia
- Japan
- Korea
- Malaysia
- Philippines
- Singapore
- Taiwan

Division II
Senior V.P.

Consumer non durables
- Unit I
- Unit II

Information systems & consumer products
- Unit I
- Unit II
- Unit III
- Services unit

Japanese business dept

Overseas branches Western Hemisphere
- Argentina
- Brazil
- Canada
- Columbia
- Mexico
- PR
- Venezuela

Division III
Senior V.P.

Overseas branches Europe, ME Asia
- Belgium
- France
- Greece
- Italy
- Netherlands
- South Africa
- Spain
- Switzerland
- UK

Division IV
Senior V.P.

Capital goods dep
- Unit I
- Unit II

Chemicals dept serv
- Unit II

Consumer durables serv
- Unit II

Metals & mining eng. serv.
- Unit II

Petroleum eng serv
- Unit II

Division V
Senior V.P.

Shipping
- N Y
- Greece
- HK
- Japan
- UK

Division VI
Senior V.P.

NCG services
- US West Coast support unit

Figure 11.5   Specialist multinational corporation unit structure

Project finance usually involves the provision of large-scale funds to governments or large (often publicly owned) institutions which brings together construction engineering and specialist equipment usually from many countries. For example, a hydroelectric project in Egypt might involve Italian construction engineering, Japanese turbines, US generators and West German steel. All of these contributors to the project may require financing in a variety of currencies in a variety of ways.

Coordinated project finance marketing will begin early during the formative stage of the project, looking for syndication possibilities for the project as a whole. At the same time liaison by country/company bank units in other countries will work with local suppliers to the project, meeting their specific needs for working capital finance, foreign exchange, and the like.

Most banks have relatively small project finance teams whose major role is in working with the overall client and/or primary contractor, arranging syndication and sharing with the normal line commercial banking officers in dealings with project suppliers. A few banks, however, have begun to formalize this liaison activity with a global network system designed to maximize penetration in particular projects.

11.5.3 Real Estate

The real estate industry is one with which the banking industry has periodic love/hate relationships. In the mid-1970s banks around the world committed a basic banking error of borrowing short to lend long to real estate developers (often undercapitalized) to finance speculative developments where expected capital profits would enable the developer to ultimately repay outstanding loans and accumulated interest. The temporary collapse of real estate values left many developers bankrupt, and many banks with heavy loan losses. As a result many banks were extremely suspicious of real estate investment by the late 1970s.

In practice the real estate market, like any other, is much more risky for the unwary and unprepared than it is to those with specialist knowledge. Further, the market can be subdivided into many sectors including:

— Short-term construction financing
— Consumer mortgage finance
— Industrial mortgage finance
— Shopping center finance
— Office finance
— Condominium finance
— Hotel and leisure complex finance

Knowledge and understanding of such markets can make the difference between success and failure.

Many banks have added real estate and mortgage specialists or subsidiaries, including construction engineers, quantity surveyors, and progress monitors to evaluate construction projects both before and during building. Successful banks tend to specialize in particular sectors and also particular geographic areas. Confidence is also developed from long-established relationships with particular developers. An example of a real estate specialist unit is shown in Figure 11.6. Many US regional banks have large real estate loan portfolios either as components of direct lending or via mortgage subsidiaries. The same function is also provided by many European banks but UK based institutions have only recently entered the mortgage market.

The involvement of many US banks in housing and property finance has been a major source of problems as the US domestic inflation rate has risen. Traditionally US mortgage lending was at fixed rates. As a result much of the US banks' domestic property portfolio has been at a fixed rate. This has in recent times been substantially lower than the bank's marginal cost of funds, which has been high due to a rising inflation rate. The savings and loans banks which specialized in mortgage lending have been under particular pressure but even major US banks have found themselves severely affected.

European banks, where they have real estate specialists, tend to have substantially fewer than their US counterparts, have few if any engineers and progress chasers, and treat such specialists as staff as distinct from line officers.

11.5.4 Energy

As with real estate, many banks have added specialists in energy and particularly oil (and more recently coal) to their commercial banking staff. The scale of lending and services to this industry is usually large and syndications are common. Evaluation of lending propositions usually requires a careful analysis of specific energy investments, while collateral may well be based on oil in the ground or the like. As a result specialist energy units may include geologists and petroleum engineers in addition to specialist account officers. Lending to the sector may also involve peripheral areas such as drilling platforms, oilfield safety equipment, offshore harbour facilities, pipeline construction, and the like.

Banks like the Texas commercial banks may well employ 100 or more officers in energy departments embracing many aspects of the industry. An example of such an energy department structure is shown in Figure 11.7. By comparison most European banks would have only a handful of specialists and these would be staff rather than line lending positions. Japanese banks have only limited in-house technical expertise but might rely on their industrial group associates in a particular industry to provide technical expertise. The lack of adequate expertise in many banks suggests that energy

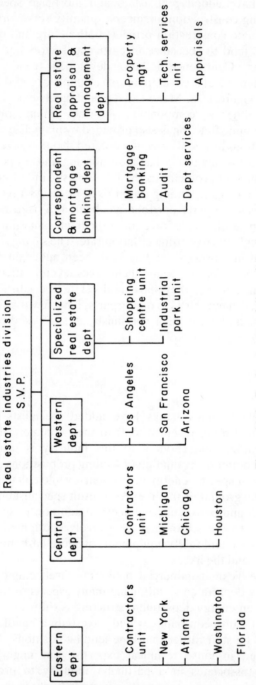

Figure 11.6 Real estate specialist unit structure

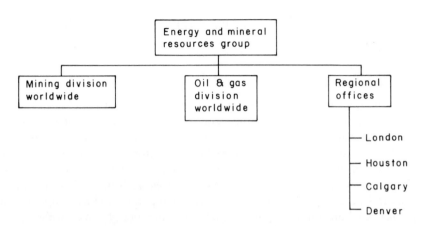

Figure 11.7   Energy and mineral resources unit structure

lending may well present similar problems for the banking industry in the 1980s as real estate did in the 1970s.

11.5.5 Commodities

Commodity markets are a more recent area for the appointment of specialist officers and the development of special products. Relatively few banks have such departments, which tend to be concentrated in major commodity market centers, notably New York, London and Chicago. An example of the organization of such a worldwide market is shown in Figure 11.8.

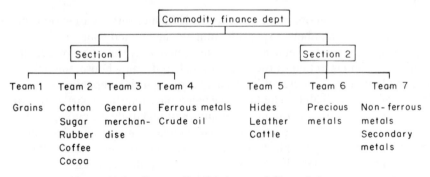

Figure 11.8   Commodity finance specialist unit structure

11.5.6 Shipping

Many banks have added shipping specialists, although like real estate this has been an area of unfortunate lending experience for several. Shipping departments are usually smaller than other major specialist sectors. Geographic concentration is normally centered upon London (handling the UK and

Scandinavia), Piraeus (dealing with the Greek market), New York, Tokyo and Hong Kong.

11.5.7 Correspondent Banking

After a number of years in the doldrums, correspondent banking has again become popular as large commercial banks perceive opportunities for deposits, transaction handling, travellers cheques, card operations and systems products. A number of major banks have therefore been gearing up their correspondent bank services, adding expertise and emphasizing joint venture cooperation. Major areas of core banking services are New York, other major domestic US cities and London. As a result separate financial institutions' organizational units have begun to emerge in a number of banks, while others treat such concerns as merely an area for industry specialization.

11.5.8 Aerospace

This speciality is not found in every bank but is a common one of West Coast US based banks, where the US aerospace companies tend to be centered. Sometimes aerospace departments also cover airline transportation companies but these are usually serviced by transportation units. The number of aerospace specialists is usually small and this speciality is less common in international banking.

11.5.9 Trade Finance

While virtually all major banks provide trade finance services of various kinds there are now a number of specialist units being created which may actually initiate trade activities and act as an intermediary. This type of activity is somewhat similar to that of the international confirming house, and indeed it seems likely that a number of banks may acquire such companies rather than developing internal units. The Japanese banks have long been part of industrial groups which invariably contain major international trading companies. These organizations are always core concerns in Japanese industrial groups and are much larger and more sophisticated than activities presently contemplated or undertaken by Western banks. Nevertheless, the development of specialist trading company units reminiscent of the Japanese concerns seems likely to be important in the 1980s both within banks and in many industrial companies. A specialist trade banking unit is illustrated in Figure 11.9.

11.5.10 Electronic Banking

The rapid growth of electronic banking in both wholesale and retail sectors is leading to the introduction of a wide range of possible fee-generating products.

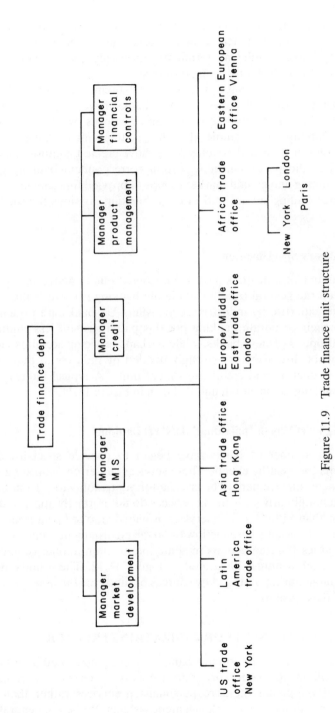

Figure 11.9   Trade finance unit structure

While operations traditionally formed the back office of the bank, the development of new products such as money management services with customer operated intelligent terminals essentially places banks in the international information processing business.

During the 1980s the range of electronic banking products is likely to increase significantly. As a result some banks have begun to split out electronic banking as a separate profit center with its own direct customer interface capability. An example of such a system unit is shown in Figure 11.10. In addition advanced systems banks have created additional information provision and processing units within correspondent banking groups, merchant banking and capital market groups to provide financial information and securities trading service and in retail banking divisions for card based services.

11.5.11 Industry Specialization

While a number of industries have been singled out as above for specialist unit attention the general trend in wholesale banking is towards the division of corporate expertise by industry sector. Many US banks are organized in this way in their corporate banking but this pattern is still less common in Western Europe. Japanese banks, while perhaps servicing accounts *via* their branch network, are also very strongly divided by industry in their central economics evaluation and credit assessment units. A typical industry-based corporate banking organization unit is shown in Figure 11.11.

11.5.12 'High Net Worth Individual' (HNWI) Banking

A substantial number of banks have begun to provide specialist service arrangements for wealthy clients. These services center on deposit gathering and investment management. The criteria for admission varies from bank to bank, but generally private banking services do not normally apply to deposit levels of less than $100,000. The services provided tend to be international in character and are usually based in low or no tax environments while providing discrete facilities for transactions in some major international centers. The structure of such a unit is illustrated in Figure 11.12. These units are also found in capital market units as key sources of funds for the asset generation activities of these groups.

11.6 TRENDS IN ORGANIZATION STRUCTURE

Competitive pressures are forcing banks to reorganize their approach to servicing medium and large corporate accounts. Even small accounts are seeing the development of more personalized services rather than being serviced by traditional branch management systems. While the general trend

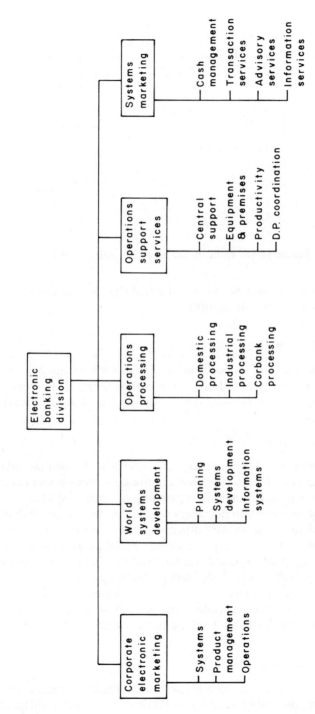

Figure 11.10 Electronic banking organization unit structure

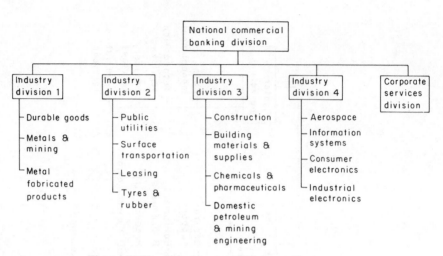

Figure 11.11   Industry specialization unit structure

will be towards customer sector based structures, within this a number of additional trends are also discernible.

Increased industry specialization

In order to provide both specialist product development and delivery and to reduce loan risks, increased industry specialization seems likely to emerge over and above the more common specialist areas which have already developed.

Increased system selling

The need to provide multiple calling on accounts with many subsidiaries or units operating in many countries will require coordination and team-selling effort. This will lead to account based planning and control systems with global account officers/relationship managers responsible for the profitability of an account overall and unit account officers responsible for their profits within their unit/country area. This type of account based planning will be a critical marketing strategy tool, especially for the small number of key accounts which will make up the bulk of wholesale bank profitability.

This team-selling approach will also tend to require coordinated multiple calling involving product specialists, notably those concerned with global money management, merchant banking and automated systems.

Specialized corporate banking

While net loan interest will continue to represent the bulk of bank earnings for the next decade, the ability of a bank to obtain credit business will increasingly

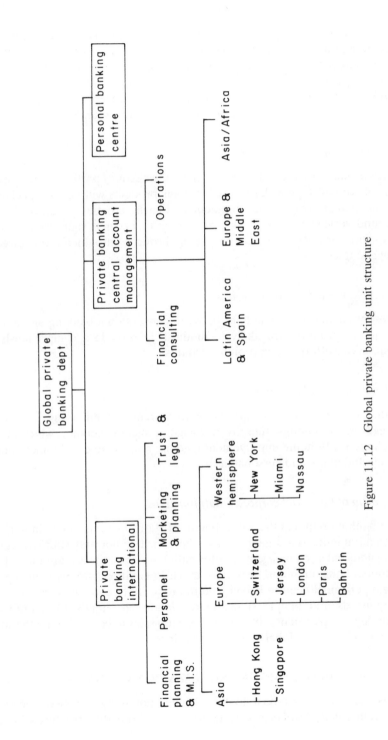

Figure 11.12 Global private banking unit structure

rely upon its ability to supply creative specialist financial services. Bank calling officers trained as credit or lending bankers will need to become more like merchant bankers, knowledgeable in a wide range of services and able to apply this knowledge to solve the financial problems of corporate treasurers. This will require substantial retraining of existing calling officers and the probable recruitment of many new executives with different backgrounds and attitudes.

Specialized product development

Specialist product packages designed to meet the needs of particular customer groups will be developed. Automated systems products will be an especially important area of product development and such activities, traditionally a background service area in banks, are likely to become significant profit centers, with operations executives being brought into increasing direct customer contact.

Integration of related banking services

The present common dividing lines between conventional banking and asset based finance products are likely to diminish to provide a comprehensive financial service offering to corporate accounts.

Specialized retail banking units

As with corporate banking, special service areas are emerging in retail banking. Notable amongst these is mortgage or shelter banking, which may well be linked with home improvement lending, real estate development and brokerage and house and personal insurance.

Development of industrial corporate staff functions

Modern banking requires the development of staff functions more similar to those found in industrial organizations. These include not only staff strategic planning units but also management information service units in addition to the conventional bank audit and inspection units. In addition, premises management and personnel need to become more proactive to cope with changes in property needs and people skills. Deregulation also tends to require a proactive legal department, able to develop strategies to cope with the threats and opportunities that global deregulation brings.

11.7 PROBLEMS OF ORGANIZATIONAL CHANGE

As banks endeavor to adjust to the changes posed by the next decade, organizational change will be necessary in order to ensure that structure adjusts to meet the needs of revised strategies. Normally, structural change occurs more by revolution than by evolution and periodic major reorganizations can be expected. However, to be successful organizational modification must take cognisance of the following factors.

Top management commitment

Without adequate commitment by top management organizational change is rarely successful since it normally involves the modification of the existing power structure. This will be resisted unless specifically supported by the leadership. As a result major reorganizations normally only occur immediately after a change in bank leadership.

Adjustment of corporate culture

Every organization has its own unique culture developed from a blend of corporate history, environment, norms and traditions, participants and leadership. Such a culture is very difficult to change. However, many banks fall into the trap of trying to emulate other organizations they feel are successful but without undertaking the necessary cultural adjustment. Again leadership change is normally a prerequisite for organization cultural change.

Retraining existing executives

The changing strategies of banks will require a different mix of people skills. Some of these can be obtained by the retraining of existing personnel but the process of achieving the desired skill changes requires training that is extensive, ongoing and carefully planned.

Adding specialist skills

The move to add new services may well require the introduction of new specialist skills such as merchant banking, project finance, energy specialists and the like. The integration of such specialists into the structure of the bank requires careful planning to ensure adequate communication and coordination.

Service integration

Growing diversity adds complexity to banking operations and increases the need to ensure that adequate organizational integration takes place. This is especially true in banks which were traditionally retail branch based operations and which have extended their international corporate interests. Great care must be taken to ensure the development of a common organizational purpose and identity and to so reduce internal rivalries.

Redundancy and unionization

Much of the change taking place in the banking industry is likely to lead to staff reductions in less skilled parts of the bank organization while additions are made to specialist skills in merchant banking and systems. While staff turnover is relatively high among such personnel enforced redundancy is likely to be required in many banks as they are forced to trim their cost structures. Few banks know how to handle such redundancies and also how to cope with the increased militancy of trade unions anxious to protect members' jobs. It is therefore important for them to develop appropriate policies in these areas to reduce the difficulties of organizational change.

11.8 SUMMARY

The form of organization adopted by a bank is an extremely important element in successful strategy implementation. A variety of organization forms can be identified and the appropriate choice of structure will depend upon the product market position of the bank. Structures are also evolving, with the continued diversification of bank services leading to changing demands on account officers and the need to introduce product managers and market segment specialists leading to the creation of market based business units.

11.9 BANK ORGANIZATION CHECKLIST

1. What is the existing organization structure of the bank?
2. Is this structure clearly consistent with the chosen product market strategy?
3. Is the present structure a function of history and the present power structure? Does this power structure need to be changed to achieve a successful customer orientation?
4. In your bank's corporate banking operations how do you compare with the key competitors along the dimensions of geography, industry and product?
5. Do you decentralize decision-making to appropriate levels to be seen as legitimate in your chosen areas of competition?
6. What mode of servicing corporate accounts has your bank chosen? Is this appropriate, and if not how can you move to change your structure and key personnel?
7. Do you have the correct level of account representation? How does your level of representation compare with competitors?
8. What specialized corporate product market segments have you specifically organized to serve?

9. Are these specialist organizational units able to match competitors in terms of quality and/or quantity of personnel?
10. Are your specialist staff units adequately developed in management information, planning and control, treasury, personnel, legal, audit, external affairs and property?
11. Are you adjusting your structure in line with changes in the marketplace and competitors?
12. Are you able to maintain appropriate expertise within the bank or do you suffer from significant labor turnover for critical skills?
13. Have you developed appropriate manpower planning, training and management succession policies to meet future bank strategic needs?
14. Have you developed appropriate rewards and sanction systems?
15. Are your recruitment procedures adequate to cope with changing personnel needs?
16. Have you developed policies for checking with trade unions, potential forced redundancy and branch closure programs?

Index

Proper names are in *Italics*

231